T0305666

Towards a Society of Degrowth

This book explores the concept of degrowth, beginning from a basic assumption, not of resource depletion, as is common in most literature in the field, but rather from a state of abundance, arguing that there is a vast amount of energy on the planet waiting to be utilized by all its inhabitants.

Adopting a sociological approach, Onofrio Romano argues that the growth momentum is not simply a broadly shared "value," but the physiological outcome of a specific institutional frame. The problem is that in its mainstream formulation the degrowth alternative shares with the growth-led regime some basic anthropological, political, and institutional pillars. In order to build a real alternative, Romano suggests reviewing degrowth in the light of the *dépense* notion by Georges Bataille. According to Bataille, our societies have no problem with acknowledging scarcity, but with dealing with the surplus energy that calls us to act for a qualified life. So, in order to erase the growth obsession, we have to ward off the "servile" dimension, i.e., the utilitarian activities needed for the mere reproduction of life, to regain sovereignty, as reflected in the de-thinking subject.

Innovative and provocative, *Towards a Society of Degrowth* will be of great interest to students and scholars of degrowth, sociology, social anthropology, political ecology, and ecological economics.

Onofrio Romano is Associate Professor of Sociology in the Department of Political Sciences at the University of Bari, Italy.

Routledge Explorations in Environmental Studies

www.routledge.com/Routledge-Explorations-in-Environmental-Studies/book-series/REES

Towards a Society of Degrowth

Onofrio Romano

LONDON AND NEW YORK

First published 2020 by Routledge

2 Park Square, Milton Park, Abingdon, Oxon OX14 4RN
605 Third Avenue, New York, NY 10017

Routledge is an imprint of the Taylor & Francis Group, an informa business

First issued in paperback 2021

Publisher's Note

The publisher has gone to great lengths to ensure the quality of this reprint
but points out that some imperfections in the original copies may be apparent.

British Library Cataloguing-in-Publication Data
A catalogue record for this book is available from the British Library

Library of Congress Cataloging-in-Publication Data
A catalog record has been requested for this book

ISBN: 978-1-138-54340-9 (hbk)
ISBN: 978-1-03-217673-4 (pbk)
DOI: 10.4324/9781351005944

Typeset in Bembo
by Wearset Ltd, Boldon, Tyne and Wear

To Serge Latouche

Contents

Foreword

Degrowthers are often blamed – regardless of whether one joins the project – for the use of the word "degrowth." It doesn't sound catchy, first of all. But the reasons for its inappropriateness are manifold. They are both substantive and tactical, and appear to be largely acceptable (as we will see later). First and foremost, the reference to the productive sphere of social life (evoked by the term "growth") – even if reversed ("degrowth") – implicitly embeds the alternative into the economic imaginary. There is no doubt, however, that by focusing on (economic) growth, the supporters of the project identify what we believe to be the most distinctive feature of Western civilization and, at the same time, the starting point of its main present drifts. In short, looking at the political marketing, it is certainly not a winning move to index "growth" and, beyond marketing, presenting a social alternative as the mere denial of economic growth is at least reductive. All true. But on the intellectual, analytical, and scientific levels the choice to focus on growth is very pertinent. At least in a twofold sense: (1) growth is a central device in modern Western societies (revealing its basic logic); (2) growth is the source of a more and more uncontrollable series of ecological, social, economic, anthropological, and political drifts that urgently demand a change of regime, a social alternative settled beyond the logic of growth. In short, growth is the (sick) heart of our civilization. The issue deserves to be placed at the center of the discussion.

Nevertheless, it is important to deeply understand the meaning of this centrality. Growth is the symptom, not the disease. It is the index pointing to the moon. Not the moon. It is the superficial exponent of a system whose logic, texture, ontology is to be discovered. The regime that produces a tension to the limitless pursuit of growth does not coincide and does not end with growth.

Moreover, growth does not benefit from political manifestos that designate it as a value in itself. Everyone talks about it, everyone pursues it, but it is difficult to identify statements of intent, charters, sacred texts that elect it as a social objective to be pursued as such. It is presented as an obvious, apodictic tension, which therefore does not need supporting arguments. Its desirability is self-evident. It appears as a "natural," unintentional attitude, independent of the sphere of values. It could be said that growth is, in a chemical and/or Paretian sense, a "residue" (Pareto, 2010). One of the basic and nonseparable components of our civilization.

Although not declared, growth represents a privileged access key to modernity. It captures its basic logic. Through growth, it is possible to access the founding constitution of Western civilization (which is a preliminary move for anyone intending to escape its yoke). Anyway, growth makes the West something new in the historical catalogue of human civilizations.

For these reasons, we cannot take it for granted that focusing on the direct effects of growth (on the environmental and social level) makes it possible to escape from the general logic from which it arises. And this is often the reduction made by degrowthers. The present work stands against this reduction. It is correct to focus our attention on growth, since it is one of the easiest access gates to the core of the dominant regime; but if we linger on the "letter," if we nominally oppose growth in itself, we cannot be sure that we will be able to defeat the "disease" of which it is only the "symptom." It is not obvious that by contrasting growth we also oppose its underlying logic.

The specificity of our contribution lies right here. This is not a book against growth and in favor of a society based on the opposite move of limiting growth or explicitly growing down. Instead, this book develops a critique of the regime that generates growth fetishism. Growth is the "symptom" of a specific anthropological, economic, social, political, and institutional "syndrome." We will discuss this syndrome here. Growth represents one of the main operating regimes of the syndrome. But this one could eventually also reject growth and manifest itself in the future under different guises, while continuing to operate and to produce damages. To put it briefly, we can get out of growth without leaving the growth regime. And, reciprocally, we can get out of the growth regime without necessarily leaving growth, the consumption of soil, resources, and energy. Theoretically, the second hypothesis seems preferable to the first.

As we will see, in fact, in many of the currently circulating degrowth narratives, growth is contested but without questioning the cornerstones of the socio-institutional regime of which it is an expression. A legitimate move (for the sake of argument, let's say it is feasible) but completely unsatisfactory, in our opinion, because it leaves untouched the factors that make our present world unlivable. Conversely, our perspective abstractly contemplates the possibility of promoting a kind of society that, although escaping from the growth regime, shows no concern about the depletion of resources and the survival of the planet (which in itself, in our opinion, is not necessarily a desirable aim), i.e., for the purposes that animate degrowth supporters. The degrowthers' main concern is to save the planet. Our concern, instead, is to live in a world that can "be loved to death" (Bataille, 1976f, 442), also accepting the possibility that it could prematurely die precisely because of our love. This goal requires leaving the "growth regime" (not necessarily growth itself). If life is the first goal for degrowthers (the search for a "good" life generally comes later, as a corollary), life itself, life for life's sake, is to us deprived of any interest. We prefer the end of the planet rather than a miserable life. For these reasons, our contribution could go beyond the boundaries within which the degrowth narrative is normally framed. We take responsibility for it. Nor do we think of degrowth as a technique of adaptation to a given fact: the alleged necessity to adapt, willingly or not, to the progressive depletion of resources (which, as we shall see, is a way to surreptitiously recover the original myth of modernity, albeit in an inverted form). We will instead start from the desirability, for human beings, of the life model generated by the growth regime.

1 The sociology of growth

Homo crescens: the anthropology of growth

Why is growth so central? Where does devotion to economic growth originate from in modern society and how is it justified? Which structure, which pattern of social life does it hide? And why is growth a deleterious logic that requires an exit strategy?

As we have already noted, growth is not, in our opinion, a "value" in the present regime. It does not represent in itself an object of pursuit on a social level. This remark is important, since framing growth in the sphere of "values" of a given social consortium is often a consolatory move that generates a strategic fault in contrasting the present regime. If growth is a value, then the battle completely shifts into the ideological field: it will be sufficient to engage in the promotion of alternative values to that of economic growth. A merely "cultural" battle. A "superstructural" struggle, I would say, if I were Marxist. It's a consolatory move, because I believe, as I will try to show here, that growth is something tougher than a simple value. It is a logic that springs from structural mechanisms, completely impermeable to values. In other words, growth is a device that cuts across the changing value structures of society in space and time. It is possible, in short, to counteract the value of growth and, hypothetically, to defeat it, without affecting the underlying "growth logic," without producing an exit from the growth regime.

To understand this mechanism, it is necessary to try for a moment to take the liberal narrative seriously. It is literally an "ideological" narrative, in the sense assigned by Marx to this adjective (Marx, 1963). The liberal narrative tends to design a specific image of society, a specific functioning regime, not as the "artificial" fruit of human choices, always changeable and revocable, but as something inscribed in "nature," something innate. This alleged naturalness, as it is known, acts as a mechanism for legitimizing a particular frame of social relations, from which the dominant classes gain privileges, consolidating their dominion over the other classes. For the liberals, the tension towards limitless self-promotion is inscribed in "nature." The subject is naturally inclined to pursue his interest without limits, in order to satisfy his needs more and more and better. Growth would therefore be a natural connotation that pertains to the anthropological constitution of the subject and that precedes any constellation of values.

To understand the foreignness of growth to the sphere of values, it is worthwhile looking at the rearticulation of the liberal discourse operated by utilitarianists, in particular by Bentham (1839). In fact, utilitarianism does not simply correspond to the limitless satisfaction of the "material" needs of the subject, assuming their primacy over all kinds of need. Bentham recognizes the multiplicity of human values and goals, affirming that the best of all possible worlds is the one that allows everyone to better pursue the goals and values autonomously selected and processed. The tension towards growth is therefore a mechanism that precedes the choice and the pursuit of values. It is a natural tendency.

This approach must be taken seriously, even if we do not share it. We do not agree, in particular, with the naturalness claim included in the narrative, i.e., the idea that the subject is a serial accumulator of utilities and that this tension is limitless and persistent in the subject. Nevertheless, we share the belief that the growth device precedes the sphere of values. It is not rooted in nature, but it is rather the outcome of a specific socio-institutional structure. If it were rooted in nature, we would have to conclude that it is not changeable and therefore we should surrender to growth. We believe instead that it stems from a particular socio-institutional structure that, of course, precedes cultural values, goals, and options, but which nevertheless has nothing that's natural or neutral, something that can be changed or undermined (and, in our opinion, has to be undermined because it is extremely harmful to humanity, rather than to the planet).

The naturalness pretense framing growth was first counteracted by sociologists. Max Weber is the author who best questioned the issue. For him, growth is certainly one of the main distinctive features (if not the main one) of "modern Western capitalism" (1947, 1992). More precisely, the tendency to a continuous and almost limitless enlargement of the productive base of the capitalist enterprise emerges as its proper character. The business profit is largely set aside (deducted from consumption) to be reinvested in the limitless increase of the original capital. This is for Weber an unheard-of mechanism in human history. One of the capitalist regime's basic features is something really new, along with the employment of a formally free workforce, with the rational organization of the productive cycle and with the centrality of market exchange. An astonishing and inexplicable feature, in many ways. Neither "rational" nor "natural," contrary to what liberal economists claimed. Before the advent of Western modern capitalism, societies produced enough to satisfy the main needs of their members. Neither more nor less. The surplus – as we will broadly see in the next chapters, talking about *dépense* – was eventually consumed in festive moments, with the prevailing aim of strengthening community ties, or was even destroyed to avoid the growth of inequalities in the distribution of resources within the community. It is only with the advent of modern Western capitalism that this paradoxical tendency to produce much more than is necessary for social reproduction in order to continuously increase the productive base manifests itself. Weber tries to comprehend this curious model of action, considering completely insufficient the "naturalistic" explanation provided by liberalism and utilitarianism. The Weberian interpretation, as it is known, could be found in *The Protestant Ethic and the Spirit of Capitalism* (1992).

Here, Weber reveals the "transcendent engine" of capitalism. It is assumed that capitalist modernity is based on immanence, on the free expression of men, on adherence to individual needs and will. Any transcendent dimension that exceeds eating and dressing is quashed. From the analytical point of view, Weber challenges this idea: "something more than mere garnishing for purely egocentric motives is involved" (1992, p. 18).

The main determinant of capitalism, its development spring, is not in the subject and his needs, but in a transcendent dimension: a faith dimension. As we know, this is a *sui generis* faith. In Protestantism, especially in its Calvinist version, the communitarian element is absent. The churchgoer establishes a form of direct communication with God. Everybody is an interpreter of scripture and needs neither intermediaries (priests), nor ecclesial communities. Weber's strong assumption is that the vocation for growth and accumulation, typical of capitalism, relies on the "predestination doctrine" of Calvinism. Of course, there is not a causal link, but rather a "structural homology" (Boudon, 1969): the form of capitalism is contiguous to Protestant doctrine. Predestination means that a man's state of grace or damnation is already established at his birth, regardless of his behavior in life. This idea generates a state of uncertainty with respect to his post-mortem condition. The inability to influence one's own destiny by earthly conduct, condemns the believer to an inextinguishable anxiety. For this reason, he desperately tries to recognize in his life some "signs" witnessing his final state in the realm of eternity. Something that attests to his salvation. Thus, success in professional life becomes a privileged sign of the state of grace. In order to self-fulfill this prophecy, Calvinists devote themselves to their professions with extreme severity. Germans call it *Beruf*, a word that means at the same time "profession" and "vocation." This is the first effect of the predestination doctrine. The believer does everything to achieve professional success, which has a tangible manifestation (a sign, in fact) in the growth of his assets. Saving and reinvesting as much as possible requires an effective and methodical conduct, always modulated on temperance. While a dissolute conduct, devoted to consumption and waste, immediately appears as a sign of damnation.

> The earning of money within the modern economic order, so long as it is done legally, is the result and the expression of virtue and proficiency in a calling…. It is an obligation which the individual is supposed to feel and does feel towards the content of his professional activity.
>
> (Weber, 1992, p. 19)

Hence, growth is the outcome of a transcendent hidden factor. More precisely, a sort of "worldly asceticism": the tension towards divinity is expressed (and this is the originality of Protestantism compared to all other religions) by a stubborn care of worldly affairs. The focus on self-interest, evoked by classical economists and liberalists, is a mere optical illusion. The tendency towards limitless growth and self-promotion has nothing to do with an alleged natural, internal, and immanent attitude of the individual, but it obeys to a specific transcendent injunction. The capitalistic society does not emanate from individuals, from their economic interests and from a general rule of free acting. "In this case the causal relation is certainly the reverse of that suggested from the materialistic standpoint" (Weber, 1992, p. 20).

Correspondingly, also admitting a generic and universal attitude to enrichment that has been manifested in previous ages, this one doesn't explain the specific features of modern Western capitalism:

> This is not wholly because the instinct of acquisition was in those times unknown or underdeveloped, as has often been said. Nor was it because the greed for gold was then, or is now, less powerful outside bourgeois capitalism than within its peculiar sphere, as the illusions of modern romanticists would lead us to believe. The difference between the capitalistic and pre-capitalistic spirit is not to be found at this point.... Absolute and conscious ruthlessness in acquisition has often stood in the closest connection with the strictest conformity to tradition
>
> (Weber, 1992, pp. 21–22)

The origin of capitalism is in a specific mentality connected with the way of life of a specific group of individuals, and this "conception of money-making as an end in itself to which people were bound, as a calling, was contrary to the ethical feelings of whole epochs" (Weber, 1992, p. 34).

The transcendental inspiration feeds earthly life, boosting growth. In the Middle Ages, on the contrary, a form of "transcendental transcendence" prevailed: religious inspiration never touched earth. God's devotees lost all contacts with worldly affairs. Or, on the contrary, the immanent communitarian dimension, typical of Catholic tradition, became overbearing, trapping the ascetic tension and diluting it in current affairs. Protestants almost unintentionally created a regime of "immanent transcendence," giving a big push to social dynamics.

> The old leisurely and comfortable attitude towards life gave way to a hard frugality in which some participated and came to the top, because they do not wish to consume but to earn, while others who wished to keep on with the old ways were forced to curtail their consumption.
>
> (Weber, 1992, p. 30)

Weber deconstructs the faith in self-interest: if it were true, probably capitalism would have never known its extraordinary growth.

It would seem that with Weber the explanation of the centrality of growth shifts from the "natural" attitude of men to the dimension of their values. The tension towards growth is explained by Protestant doctrine. Then, only afterwards, this specific cultural input is generalized (and it evaporates) thanks to the almost automatic functioning of capitalism that always seeks new ways of exploitation, colonizing new spaces, even those untouched by Calvinist prophecy. But, looking closely, Weber refers to an "ontological" dimension of humankind, that has a psychological manifestation: the desire for existential reassurance, i.e., the conquest of salvation. This motive resonates with a particular structure of the Calvinist doctrine, and it then generates a particular state of anguish from which the tension for growth springs. This is only the original momentum: after which, as mentioned above, capitalism develops almost mechanically.

In short, to explain growth, according to Weber, the natural impulse to self-promotion, to the limitless pursuit of the satisfaction of one's own needs and to the realization of one's own interests is not enough. There is a deeper impulse to explain growth, i.e., the search for the eternal salvation as a remedy for the unbearable mortality. The fact that, in the capitalist age, this universal feeling of anxiety for salvation translates in a growth tension (a functional substitute for the old religious consolations) is due, according to Weber, to a specific religious narrative. So, the basic drive for growth is no longer a natural (and universal) attitude but the specific values constellation established in Northern Europe at the dawning of the modern age.

This conclusion is, in our opinion, unsatisfactory. Weber's hypothesis certainly explains the "exceptional" devotion to growth shown by Protestant societies at the origins of capitalism, but it is not sufficient to explain the "general" growth tension that frames modern society as a whole, at any latitude and throughout its historical development, beyond the specific Calvinist momentum.

In our opinion, the growth attitude is neither natural, nor responds to a pattern of values. Instead, it springs from a specific institutional order. It is the outcome of a particular social structure, or better relational order between institutions, individuals, and nature. Namely, it is the effect of "individualization."

This leads us to the heart of our argument. The anguish generated by uncertainty about our otherworldly destiny is not channeled towards growth because of the contents and of the structure of Protestant ethics: this unheard-of solution basically derives from a new institutional background, coeval to the spread of Protestantism. Nevertheless, it is true that Protestantism has provided a fundamental contribution to the emergence of the new institutional conditions.

As Merton (1963, 1996) points out, Protestantism was born as a challenge to the Church: by attempting to the ecclesial authority it promotes the erasing of all mediation between the believer and God. This big thrust towards individualization is at the origins, as it is well known, of the scientific attitude. Therefore, regardless of the content of the Protestant doctrine, its most disruptive social consequences derived from the historical circumstances in which it was forged. The stimulus towards individualization generated the growth attitude. From the "horizontalized" structure of society (also due to the anti-institutional genesis of Protestantism) the tension to limitless growth springs out, bouncing off the Calvinist doctrine of predestination. It is not a purely cultural issue, but an institutional trait.

So growth, in our opinion, is not a value among others that miraculously gains hegemony in our societies after an ideological–cultural struggle, but it is the effect of the fundamental structural connotation of modernity, that is the break of the communitarian cohesion and the progressive emancipation of the single particles making up the whole. The tension towards growth is the basic result of individualization. Any attempt to escape from the growth regime that does not touch the individualized structure of modern society is doomed to failure, even when armed with the best intentions, even when it is endowed with a cultural envelope (values, conscience, etc.) that harshly opposes the limitless growth trajectory.

On this point, some of Bataille's lines, to which we will often return, appear to be particularly enlightening, helping to immediately frame the first effect (in terms of tension on limitless growth) of the gaze "particularization" generated by modernity:

> as a rule, *particular* existence always risks succumbing for lack of resources. It contrasts with *general* existence whose resources are in excess and for which death has no meaning. From the *particular* point of view, the problems are posed *in the first instance* by a deficiency of resources. They are posed *in the first instance* by an excess of resources if one starts from the *general* point of view.
>
> (1988, p. 39)

The individualized being is bound by the precarious nature of his existence and therefore obsessed with the problem of his survival. When isolated, he embraces a fundamentally servile vocation and reverts to the status of an animal, for which obtaining resources is crucial.

The material obsession does not derive from a real shortage of resources available to the actor, but it is a sort of optical effect induced by the condition of individualization in which modernity puts him. The loss of contact with the community's protective umbrella places the individual in a condition of structural precariousness, so that he feels obliged to act limitlessly for his own survival. He permanently feels in a state of emergency for life, which leads him to never give up the effort of accumulating resources even when they become more than enough to ensure him a dignified life. This is not a "natural" condition; it is not an innate instinct to pursue one's own interest (as liberals and utilitarians postulate); it is not the true face of the human being. It is an attitude that stems from a specific structuring of the relationship between actor and society, which specifically emerges in the modern era. Nor is it a "real" historical condition of scarcity, which rationally justifies the tension towards the accumulation of resources and utility. The quantity of goods owned by the *homo crescens* at a given moment is completely irrelevant for his general attitude. He doesn't quiet down with the acquisition of resources. The anxiety leading him to accumulate more and more is independent of his material well-being, because this attitude derives exclusively from the institutional condition in which he operates. And it is also independent from his values and his rule of life. The tension towards growth cuts across the whole value constellation inside the horizontal and individualizing institutional set-up.

In *The Civilizing Process* (1969), Norbert Elias deals with the genesis of the "society of individuals" (1990). Here we find an unsurpassed sociohistorical reconstruction of the process that led to the progressive emancipation of the actor from his communitarian context.

According to the German sociologist, structural changes in society are closely connected with the structural change of the individual psyche and, on this basis, he explains the strong interrelation between individualization and rationalization.

Medieval communities were, from the administrative, social, and economic point of view, almost independent one of each other. They had few relations between them, and men integrally spent their life in the limited horizon of their small circles. In these units, between the community and its single members there is a seamless relationship. The member doesn't perceive himself as something separate from the community and he doesn't even imagine himself outside it: "the isolated individual, the individual without a group didn't have many chances to survive" (Elias, 1990, p. 201). In the economy of his psychological drives there are no unexpressed residues, since due to the absence of individual boundaries he cannot perceive the possible presence of impulse energies enclosed within these boundaries: there is a kind of holism, or osmosis between the individual and the community. The latter functions as a whole, with no autonomy of its single parts. The single member is an immediate expression of what Elias calls "social habitus": he is totally informed by the symbolic communitarian universe in which he lies:

> in the first, smaller and more compact formations, the most important role for the regulation of individual behavior relies on the constant presence of the others, on the continuous coexistence with the others, the consciousness of the never ending and indissoluble affinity with the others and, not least, on direct fear of the others. So the individual has not the chance, the need, nor the capacity to be lonely.
>
> (Elias, 1990, p. 149)

So, the single actor is always under the communitarian umbrella. Regardless of the specific economic conditions, he always feels at one with the collective body which he belongs to. He is not directly confronted with the environment, so his life does not exclusively depend on his personal ability to self-extract resources. His fusion in the communitarian organism keeps him away from the concern and the activation effort for the satisfaction of his survival needs. There's no need to unleash dynamism.

Living in a very small community, with a limited horizon, the single actor personally knows the members of his group; the glue between them is created by daily narrowness, where the affective ingredient is central. The subject is not requested to curb his passions, because these do not compromise the life of the group. On the contrary, this life is often protected just by the external-ization, in due time, of aggressive impulses. It is in this emotional confusion between subject and group, where the same affection ownership is lost, that the sense of the priority assigned to the We-identity resides, in spite of the I-identity. The individual does not perceive any distance between him and the members of his group, between him and the objects that surround him: his potential identity is integrally diluted and reabsorbed in the organic rela-tion between him and the others, between him and the objects. So, the actor's energy is structurally catalyzed and reabsorbed by the community: he has no possibility to freely plunder the environment, based only on his needs and desires. The result is a sort of steady state.

More than any other, David Riesman (1950) has highlighted the strong connection between the breakdown of this kind of aggregation, the resulting individualization and "growth." He assigns a central place to the demographic variable. This is undoubtedly the most controversial and contested point of his theory. Edgar Morin, in the preface to the French edition of the work (Morin, 1971) underlines the high degree of epistemological roughness included in this hypothesis of direct causality between demographic evolution and social change.

Western demographic evolution could be graphically represented on the Cartesian axes by an "S" curve. The horizontal line at the base describes a situation of population invariance: the very numerous births are counter-balanced by equally numerous deaths. This configures a stage of "high growth potential."

Around the 17th century, a fundamental change occurred: due to the growth of food production and to the better general hygiene conditions, the mortality index rapidly decreases. The population starts to dramatically grow. A real demographic explosion occurs, represented by the "S" vertical line.[1] We are now in the "transitional growth" stage.

The birth rate conspicuously slows down during the 20th century: it is the dawning of the demographic decline (what Riesman calls the stage of "incipi-ent population decline"), represented by the "S" upper horizontal line. A new phase of very slow population growth starts.

According to Riesman, each one of these demographic stages corresponds to a particular type of society, which imposes on its members some specific requisites of psychosocial conformity. In the stage of high growth potential, the social balance is assured by the individual's attitude of faithfully following the dictates of tradition: so, we will have "tradition-directed" subjects. The society arising from the transitional growth stage is mainly based on the self-determination of its members; stability is here assured by the tendency of individuals to quickly choose a set of well-defined aims coming from a personal elaboration and to be pursued throughout their lives. They are the so-called inner-directed individuals. The last stage – i.e., "transitional growth" – coincides with the coming of the "other-directed" type of conformity: i.e., the individual is now mainly moved by a peculiar tendency to search for the approval of others. Our interest here is about the passage from the tradition-directed to the inner-directed type of conformity.

Societies facing the high potential growth stage live in a condition of relative equilibrium, due the balance between births and deaths. The effect is a stabilization of mores and a substantial absence of stimulus for dynamism and social change. So, we witness a multisecular sedimentation of the communitarian structures and of the inherited symbolic order: the individual is not solicited to produce innovation inside the fixed frame of norms where he lives. He just has to conform to it and to reproduce its instances. He is integrally reabsorbed in a tight plot of social values and his actions have an eminently prescriptive nature, since all the replies to the possible situation are offered in advance by the conventional pervasive models. The individual organically belongs to his communitarian circle, such as the family, the clan, the caste, the village, and he doesn't have access to the level of self-consciousness that allows him to perceive himself as a discrete entity.

The transitional growth phase, namely the age of "growth," produced by the fall of the mortality rate, brings society into an emergency condition, with unheard of necessities, in relation to which the reiteration of the traditional cultural models proves inadequate. Communitarian behavioral codes do not provide answers on the matter: it is henceforth necessary to autonomously contrive unprescribed ways of action, to be ready with new action schemes to face the multiple, unprecedent problems that arise, time by time. Penury, lack of resources, etc. are the priorities, due to the population growth. All efforts and interventions converge on the economic emergency. In these conditions, society needs a new type of conformity of its members, with unique features: namely, the inner-directed individual, whose privileged determination source is located inside himself. This subject can no more indulge in the static game of the mere reproduction of the patterns used by his group, nor he can be guided by his natural impulses, by his passing attitudes to immediately satisfying his desires; due to penury, he has to achieve a "penury mentality," i.e., he must put aside the symbolic communitarian injunctions and spontaneous attitudes in order to focus on the resolution of the material problem, on the effort for valorizing the existing resources. Sahlins (1974), in this sense, defines the primitive communities as abundance societies: here, the material problems are not in the foreground. The objects do not have a merely useful value, but first of all a symbolic value. Modern societies, although incomparably richer than the archaic ones, are based on a penury mentality and on the continuous tension generated by an alleged and always incumbent scarcity of resources.

With a well-fitting metaphor, Riesman assimilates the psychological mechanism that drives the inner-directed individual to a "gyroscope," i.e., an instrument that allows him to always hold the route towards the aims elected by himself, despite the temptations of instinct and the reversed solicitations coming from the external world. The inner-directed subject does not have in front of him an already traced path: he embraces aims and aspirations that overcome the immediate situation and that imply, above all, a personal choice, i.e., a high dose of self-consciousness of his means: he acts like a pioneer, always exploring new frontiers, particularly in the production realm, moved by an iron will that prevents relaxing and disengagement. He creates and consciously transforms his world on the basis of an autonomous long-term project, a general aim, a value to which he assigns supreme relevance, without adapting himself to the inherited structures. Thanks to these individual features, the resulting society undertakes a strong transformation dynamics.

Individualization produces a new public sphere. The individual tends to build himself beyond the principle of social coerciveness. He aspires to meet the collective dimension only after the constitution of the self, so postulating a contractual and deliberate foundation of the social sphere, with which he doesn't have an organic relationship and from which he feels separate. In this sense, with the imaginary institution of the individual, at the same time what we call "society" arises, replacing the mere sociality typical of the traditional communities. Modernity tends to abolish all the intermediate bodies that hinder a fully universal unity (Tönnies, 1963).

This "view from afar" of the evolution that has produced the consolidation of the new social order is certainly contestable, mainly for its demographical reductionism and for its peculiarly materialistic setting. Nevertheless, it provides a very stimulating version about the origins of the growth regime, developed at the dawning of industrial modernity. It very vividly explains why the subjects move away from the community and start to act alone, according to their personal strategies, why they rationalize their behavior and why they are so absorbed in the aim of economic growth.

The succeeding shift to "other-directedness," during the 20th century, is a sort of reversion towards premodern community. But this return to the search for the communitarian warmth (in the new guises provided by mass culture, electronic media, and consumerism) is locked up inside the borders of the cultural dimension and doesn't really touch economic life. As Daniel Bell (1976) asserts, in advanced capitalistic society we witness a clear-cut separation between economics and culture. The former continues to be framed by the prerequisite values of protestant ethics (calculation, rationalization, maximization of profit, propensity to save and reinvest, tendency to limitless growth, etc.), the latter becomes the realm of pleasure, laziness, feeling, hyperconsumption, and so on. The contradiction is only superficial, because the one dimension feeds the other.

But let's come back to Elias, in order to better specify the sense of individualization in the growth age. The opening of the communitarian organism towards the outdoors and its integration in larger and larger territorial units has not to be confused with the granting to the individuals of the freedom to move autonomously and without responding to any central authority. Social functions begin to differentiate, and men start to depend on a larger and larger number of other men with whom they have to align their actions, then the subject necessarily has to respond to new adaptation mechanisms:

> The individual is forced to regulate his behavior, making it more and more differentiated, more regular, more stable.... The interweaving of actions becomes so complicated and wide, the tension imposed by the necessity to "correctly" behave becomes so strong that in man, beside conscious self-control, a blind and automatic self-control device also arises.... Consciously or not, the orientation of this behavioral modification toward an always more differentiated regulation of the whole psychic system is fostered by social differentiation , by the progressive division of functions and by the widening of the interdependence chains, inside which, directly or indirectly, every motion, every manifestation of the individual is inserted.
>
> (Elias, 1969, pp. 642–643)

The individualized subject, separating himself from the communitarian mixture, has paradoxically to respond to a very binding set of injunctions coming from the newly arising social space. Individualization is invariably accompanied by a huge "rationalization" of behavior: the contrary of spontaneity.

The original unit inside which man's life is exhausted irretrievably falls apart. Now, the capacity to adequately insert, with well-selected, differentiated, and calibrated acts, in a wide cycle of actions assures his survival. This necessarily requires a strong effort towards temperance: in the new situation, indulging in passions, losing self-control, remaining attached to the symbolic injunctions of the community means to compromise the functioning of the whole cycle of actions and to jeopardize his own life at the same time.

Together with this movement of integration and differentiation, a complementary movement is triggered: central administrative institutions that watch over the new and broader territorial units monopolize the physical coercion. The interaction space must be pacified in order for the interdependence circuits to become denser and wider. So, individuals are prevented from using force personally: now only the central institutions are enabled to employ physical coercion and exclusively under well-defined and specific circumstances. In the new pacified areas "the individual is widely protected against attacks, against a brutal use of physical force; but at the same time he is forced, in his turn, to repress the explosion of his passions, the aggressive impulses against the other" (Elias, 1969, p. 646). The violent impulses are segregated in the backstage of consciousness.

> Repression of spontaneous aggressiveness, affects control, mental horizon widening in order to embrace the previous and the subsequent chain of effects, these are all different features of one behavioral transformation, and precisely the one that arises in coincidence with the monopolization of the power to exert physical violence and with the widening of action chains and of interdependences in social space.
>
> (Elias, 1969, pp. 646–647)

To illustrate the sense of the double structural change – social and psychical – Elias compares the attitude differences that the individual must employ when he has to cross, on the one hand, the bumpy paths of a still-not-peaceful countryside or, on the other, the trafficked streets of a modern metropolis. In the first case, the main source of fear for the subject is the possibility of suffering an attack, by a beast or by another man: under these conditions, his survival chances depend on his capacity to give vent, in due course, to his aggressiveness, to exert violence against his aggressor. In the second situation, the main risk for the individual is that someone (or himself) loses control of his impulses, that he doesn't duly respect the traffic light indications, the speed limits, the mandatory street directions, the lane delimitations: if he is not able to transform the external constraints (here materialized by the road signs) into self-constraints, if he is not able to get his impulses under control, his life and that of others will be exposed to grave danger.

> Now reflection, the precision attitude, temperance, a more rigorous emotions regulation, the knowledge of the fellows and of the whole social field become the necessary prerequisites of any social success.... Pleasure and the passing inclinations are repressed, as we are able to foresee our suffering if we surrender to them.
>
> (Elias, 1969, pp. 685–686)

Rationalization of behavior is, at the same time, the instrument that makes the new form of regulation work, based on the autonomy of the single units of the system, and its heavier consequence on the anthropological plane.

> The firmer, comprehensive and uniform control on the emotions that characterizes this sliding of civilization, the growing self-constraints that inexorably curb all the most spontaneous impulses and prevent them from directly and visibly driving the actions, without any interference by control apparatus, all this is experienced like in a cage, like an invisible wall that separates the "internal world" of the individual from the "external world," or also the knowledge subject from the objects, the ego from the other, the individual from society; and the contents are the instinctive

and affective impulses, whose access to the musculoskeletal system is prevented.

(Elias, 1969, p. 85)

In order to gain self-consciousness, to create himself knowingly and so be able to respond to the new differentiated and integrated social situation with a proper behavior, the individual must break the osmosis relation with his community, he has to ban any affective implication and he has to look "rationally" at what surrounds him.

> The passage at the perception of nature as a landscape with respect to the observer, as a knowledge object that is separated by an invisible wall from the observer, the passage to a more intense self-experience of each person as an individual, entirely founded on his own, independent and separated from other men and things, this and other phenomena typical of the age bear the characteristics of a same civilization turning.
>
> (Elias, 1969, pp. 85–86)

The two narratives (the one by Riesman, the other by Elias) seem to be incompatible. Riesman designs an individual who all alone leaves the community in search of new ways to satisfy his needs. Elias portrays the escaped individual as a ring in a long chain. The narratives are both true. Modernity is now described as the epic of the individual, then as the realm of total institutions, large and heavy, which swallow the individual in their organizational coils. From our point of view, the result doesn't change. First, the member of the collective body becomes aware of his singularity and he rationalizes his behavior. Second (and this is our major concern here), the new order generates a marked tension towards economic growth: both by individual mobilization fed by the sense of emergency for life, and by social differentiation parallel to the action chains elongation, the capacity of men to exploit the environment for their needs shows an extraordinary enhancement. The new extended social organization doesn't work on the basis of a symbolic order. It's an anonymous and abstract order, a real "machine," only driven by the logic of efficiency and totally indifferent to specific individuals or social values. Nothing to share with the old, premodern community.

The tendency towards growth fundamentally springs from the centrality taken by the "use value," as a consequence of individualization, i.e., from the direct link between the subject and the object. The emancipation of the subject implies, in fact, a contextual emancipation of the object from the communitarian grammar. As Jean Baudrillard explains:

> there is a homology between the emancipation, in the bourgeois age, of the private individual whose aims are determined by his needs, and the functional emancipation of the objects over their use value.
>
> (1972, p. 158)

The sense of the object, as the sense of the individual and of all entities, is no longer socially defined. The community no longer coercively determines the value of things. Objects are deprived of their grammatical structure, i.e., the coherent set of codified differences inside which they base their position and specific value. In the gift exchange, for instance, the object bears a social tie, "it is inseparable from the concrete relation where it is exchanged, from the transferential pact that it seals between two persons: so it has not become autonomous as such" (Baudrillard 1972, p. 61). It is always marked – like the myth – by the ambiguity of the manifestation of the desire for union between the donor and the donee, and by the contemporary attestation, through the same gift, of an unbridgeable distance between the two, if not of a real repulsion: "medium of the relation *and* of the distance, the gift is always love and aggression" (Baudrillard, 1972, p. 62). Relieved of this symbolic function or abstracted from the recognized communitarian grammar, the object was simply insignificant.

The "individualized individual," whose main psychological exercise coincides, as we have said, with the bracketing of the group injunctions, aspires to build a direct and immediate relationship with the object. He expects to find in it a pure, "objective" value, which transcends any symbolic burden, anyway considered as a form of hiding its authentic substance.[2]

For this aim, it is necessary to find a new criterion for the meaning elaboration based upon the abstract individual; a new element that intercedes between the individual and the object is necessary, building an "objective" relationship. Here "the ideological genesis of need" (Baudrillard, 1972) takes place and the individual is reduced to a "subject of needs." The "need," considered as a physiologically innate fact in the individual – emerging beyond and before any social input – becomes the necessary *trait d'union* between the subject and the object: through it, it is possible to assign to the object an "objective" function and so recognize in it a substantial value beyond its symbolic *maquillage*.

> This hypothesis ... assigns a functional statute to the objects, i.e., the tool statute linked to the technical operations over the world and the mediation statute in relation to the "natural" anthropological needs of the individual In this perspective, the objects are firstly functional to the needs and take their meaning close to the economic relation between man and the environment.
>
> (Baudrillard, 1972, pp. 7–8)[3]

The authentic criterion in order to determine the object's meaning is now "use value," i.e., its economic usefulness, its fitness in satisfying subjective needs.

> Use value ... doesn't appear as a social relation ... usefulness *as such* ... designates an objective relation with its own unmasked finalization and

whose transparence challenges history; *as a form* ... as a useful value, the object achieves abstract universality, "objectivity" (by reduction of all symbolic function).

(Baudrillard, 1972, pp. 155, 157)

In this way, objects also become measurable, comparable with each other and sortable in a value scale.[4] Economic usefulness becomes the universal ruling principle of the relation between nature and the individual.

The ideological genesis of need does not only imply the deletion of any symbolic function of the object and its reduction to a mere commodity, but it also implies, on another side, the reduction of the individual to his alleged natural needs.[5] Since the desires, the motivations and the meaning of the individual are no longer the manifestations of the coercion exerted by the community, the individual recognizes his pure essence, beyond the social domain, in his own needs: they become a new form of determination, rationally identifiable, and not vitiated by the symbolic burden. If the object truth is now exclusively in its use value ("the usefulness principle becomes the reality principle of the object" –Baudrillard, 1972, p. 156), the subject truth is, correspondingly, in his needs:

In fact, we can summarize defining the subject by the object and *vice versa*: it is a giant tautology, where the concept of need is the consecration.

(Baudrillard, 1972, p. 70)

The abstract social individual (the "needs" man), is the man thought in terms of use value.

(Baudrillard, 1972, p. 157)

For these reasons, in modern societies, the economic dimension achieves a privileged position, compared to the others. The personal realization of the individual coming out of the individualization process is substantially identified with his economic growth, with his increasing capacity to satisfy his needs.[6] So his privileged activity, through which, it is assumed, he acquires full self-affirmation, his authentic freedom and his dignity coincides with productive activity. He realizes himself through work:

the individual, released from any collective obligation of a magic or religious nature, "freed" from his archaic, symbolic or personal ties, finally "privatized" and autonomous, defines himself by an "objective" nature-transforming activity – labor – and by the destruction of useful values for his profit: needs, satisfactions, use value.

(Baudrillard, 1972, p. 158)

So, the fulfillment of human being is now identified by the production and the consumption of use values, potentially limitless. Here lies the social legitimation of growth.

In this key, we find insufficient the Marxian critique of the "exchange value" as the main drive of alienation (Marx, 1973, 1990). Certainly, the circumstance that capitalists produce fundamentally for the market marks a detachment of the production sphere from the human consortium and it triggers a tendency towards growth for growth's sake (i.e., capitalistic enterprises do not produce for the satisfaction of their operators' needs, but for the purpose of profit, in itself). But the return to the "use value," assuming it will be possible, would not produce a release from the growth obsession, for the reasons explained above. This is why Marxian thought remains trapped in the growth regime.

As we can see, modernity is profoundly marked by the centrality of materialism, not only because of the emergency trait (Riesman) but also because, due to the in the individualistic bubble in which he is closed, the subject witnesses the amplification of the material concern (see Bataille); he almost exclusively identifies the value with the "use value" that refers to individual needs (Baudrillard) and also the existential anxiety for mortality translates, through the filter of Calvinist doctrine, into an individual challenge for material growth. But the logic of growth is not confined in the material sphere. Individualization of the social regime leads to marrying a limitlessness logic even in the moral sphere. Growth thus reveals as an impulse that transcends any specific dimension of society, emerging instead as a general device, that is the direct fruit of individualization.

The narratives, recounted above, on individualization suggest that change in the relationship between the individual and the community does not respond to a political "project" or to a philosophical intention. It rather appears as an accident, an unintentional consequence of other historical events (life urgency due to the demographic imbalance or the integration of medieval communities into ever-wider and more peaceful spaces, etc.). Once subtracted from communitarian fusion, once "brought to light" as a conscious entity, the individual progressively stands as a sovereign dominus, aiming at deliberately forging the context around him on the basis of autonomously elaborated value options. The truth about the world is not already given. It is not up to tradition, God, or the community. Man realizes that he can autonomously build the truth about the world and then forge, on this ground, his own existence. Magatti (2009) has properly redefined modernity as a regime characterized by individual freedom in the search for truth. When individualized, the research effort becomes limitless and reversible at any moment: truth cannot be revealed once and for all, if it is acknowledged as the outcome of an individual elaboration and it is no longer believed to be the revelation of an extra-human powerful entity. This circumstance triggers off a trajectory of moral limitlessness, very similar to the growth injunction. It is the same action scheme reproducing itself in all social fields, which relates to the same structural cause.

A neutralitarian regime: the political institutions of limitless growth

Around the *homo crescens*, a specific institutional casing is then built: the "neutralitarian regime."

This regulation system responds to a general paradigm, i.e., a complex scheme that contains both a specific look at reality and a political and action model: the general form, the basic framework that orders our knowledge of reality (social theory), on the one side and, on the other, our collective existence (social institutions). The neutralitarian regime originally frames into a horizontalist paradigm (Romano, 2014).

For horizontality, immanence is the privileged dimension. To understand society, we must first refer to individuals and their relational strategies. In general, it is believed that we can find the true meaning of a social organism by looking at its single players and the networks they interweave with. The order doesn't radiate from a central control room, but it is the *ex post* result of the interaction dynamics between social actors. The single parts may be independent of one another, or meld according to common principles. In any case, they do not respond to a central intentionality.

The analytical level is also linked to the political manifestation.[7] Here the dominant narrative sounds more or less like this: a social order is much more desirable insofar as it leaves out the subject "as is," promoting a process of self-revelation. "Let it be" is the motto. Individuals must be what they prefer to be. The more social players are free to act and interact based upon their own preferences, the more society as a whole will be happy. The acephalous logic is seen as the most proper to understand social life and, consequently, to steer society.

Both on the analytical and normative levels, the horizontal view is led to imagine the existence of a sort of basic region, alien to any institutional form, where "authenticity" lies. In Marxist terms (Marx, 1973), this region is an infrastructural domain, with respect to which everything must be considered as a derived superstructure. It imagines that the molecules and the singularities swarming in this grassroots dimension have an original character that needs to transpire and to emerge: any attempt to steer these molecules from outside is not only impracticable, but also abusive and immoral. There is a kind of spontaneity of social life that has to be left alone, to the free will of its parts. What is the original unit inside this dimension? It depends on the schools of thought and political options. For liberalism, the fundamental unit is made up of individuals. For other traditions, it is the micro-relational environment (i.e., the proximity–affective community) in which the "person" flourishes, as against social organization (Donati, 2012). If the identification of the individual as the original unit leads immediately to elect the market as the most proper institutional order, in the relational approach the motto is: "neither with the State nor with the market." The golden dimension is the self-governing grassroots community that comes before individuals and well before public institutions and their ruling pretensions.

Horizontality appears to be the "natural" order, more harmonious and suited to individual moods. Sorokin, in this respect, talked about the "sensate" form of integrated culture, as opposed to the "ideational" one (1985, pp. 25–28).[8] In the sensate frame, reality is only that which is presented to the sense organs (it does not seek any supersensory reality). Reality is thought as a becoming, a process, a constant change, a flux, an evolution, a progress, a transformation. Human needs and aims are mainly physical and subjects are in a constant search for maximum satisfaction. For these aims the external world can be exploited either in an "active" logic (efficient modification, adjustment, readjustment, reconstruction of the external milieu) or in a "passive" mood (parasitic exploitation and utilization of the external reality as it is, viewed as the mere means for enjoying sensual pleasures), or even in a "cynical" way (that is, a sensate way masked by ideational inspiration).

The push to growth is then a natural outcome. Acemoglu and Robinson (2012) provide the most exhaustive explanation of how socioeconomic development is naturally triggered by the adoption of "inclusive institutions," that is a regulation system allowing the greatest possible acting freedom to the elementary particles of society (mainly individuals).

Self-regulating market is the "exchange model" (or the form of integration) that more faithfully translates horizontalism, according to Polanyi (2001). It is the central pivot around which, in the 19th century, the Western countries' prevailing institutional pattern developed. This feature is unheard of in the history of humankind. Market exchange always flanked the other exchange models studied by Polanyi, i.e., "reciprocity," "redistribution," and "householding." But it never appeared as the main and dominant institutional pattern. The self-regulating market is the regime in which "instead of the economy being embedded in social relations, social relations are embedded in the economic system" (Polanyi, 2001, p. 60). All human societies have an economic dimension, but none has ever been an "economic society." The reduction of the factors of production – labor, land, and money – to mere commodities, like any other, authorizes this conclusion.

The single elements melded with the communitarian aggregates of the Middle Ages embark on a process of "disembedding." They are progressively released from their communitarian sets. They start to move like separate entities, on the basis of autonomous strategies and leaving aside any central direction. The whole they belong to is now only an abstract totality, without identity and without any project, in which the principle of authority is replaced by a neutral form of regulation, being passive in front of the individual trajectories: the output is an inextricable network of interdependencies. The multiple institutions and authorities that weigh down the individual are replaced by a sole regulative infrastructure – i.e., the market rule.

The relations of master, journeyman, and apprentice; the terms of the craft; the number of apprentices; the wages of the workers were all regulated by the custom and rule of the guild and the town. What the mercantile system did was merely to unify these conditions either through statutes as in England, or through the 'nationalization' of the guilds as in France.

(Polanyi, 2001, p. 73)

Land also remained *extra commercium*, in England as in France (till 1789). The status and the function of land were determined by legal and customary law.

These bonds prevented the circulation of the factors of production (land and labor above all), without which a self-regulated market and the capitalistic valorization cannot exist.

Under feudalism and the guild system land and labor formed part of the social organization itself (money has yet hardly developed into a major element of industry).

(Polanyi, 2001, p. 72)

The Reformation in England also played in favor of land marketization. Starting from the 16th century, Church properties were first confiscated, then assigned to royal favorites and finally sold to speculators at low prices.

One of the crucial passages towards the dissolution of the corporate bonds inside the communities and the loss of their economic autonomy was undoubtedly the complex event of the common land enclosures, which started in England in the 15th century. The landowning aristocracy began the enclosures under the impulse of the strong wool price rise, due to the growth of Flemish wool manufacture. The feudal lords uprooted large numbers of the peasantry, forcibly driving them from their land. Arable land was turned into pasture, which only require a few herdsmen. This conversion drove large masses of people to abandon households and rural areas.

The institutional innovations provided by the French Revolution were, in their turn, decisive for the setting up of the horizontalist regime. They were first advocated by the Declaration of Human and Citizen's Rights and then promoted by the Constitution of 1791. The principle of equality of citizens in the participation in law formation is, in itself, a powerful individualization device that deconstructs social hierarchies. The statute of the subject is no longer determined by the fact of belonging to a specific social circle, but it directly emanates from citizenship, guaranteed by the State.

The new Constitution was characterized by a strong thrust against all the intermediate social bodies interposed between the individual and the State. Not only the feudal privileges and the craft guilds were abolished but any similar form of association. Even the aggregations aimed at mutual aid or benevolence were outlawed or subjected to rigid controls, as they competed on matters where the exclusive State competence was deployed. The religious orders suffered the same fate and ecclesiastical assets were confiscated.

"Liberté du travail" (the freedom of work) is clearly enshrined. By itself, it embodies one of the fundamental conditions for the development of the capitalistic enterprise, i.e., as we have seen with Weber, the availability of a "formally free" mass of workers.

Even marriage was integrally retrieved under the juridical form of the "contract," so underlining the exclusive competence of the single consorts on the matter, in spite of the families' alliance strategies.

Under this logic ranks the principle of the forced partition of the inheritance that contributes to the decomposition of family assets: many properties and lands, in this way, become available for market exchange and enter the cycle of capitalistic valorization.

Between 1830 and 1840 a set of reforms inspired by the utilitarian doctrine of Jeremy Bentham was introduced, in strong opposition to the inspiration of the Poor laws.[9] These reforms sanctioned the final marketization of land and labor.

> A market economy is an economic system controlled, regulated and directed by market prices; order in the production and distribution of goods is entrusted to this self-regulating mechanism.
>
> (Polanyi, 2001, p. 71)

On the institutional side, more properly, the neutralitarian regime endorses the logic of "limitless accessibility" (Romano, 1993, 2008). Authority should not express and realize a specific life ideal. It just enables citizens to design and realize their own life project. It is possible to reinterpret the history of the modern era as a progressive disclosure of the opportunities for the human being to show his poietic capabilities.

At the philosophical level, the most original legitimation source of this decree lies in the effort to "humanize the truth" undertaken by the modern philosophy founder, Descartes (Husserl, 2000). The apodictic *ego*, operator of the methodical doubt, is the only entity that cannot be denied, i.e., it is not susceptible of a suspension by the skeptical *epoché* procedure: on this basis the limitless citizenship of values, symbolic forms, meanings is legitimated as multiple manifestations (although never definitively opted) by which going back to the unique "human essence." Anything is deniable except the *ego*. Here the philosophical universalism, coined by the Greeks, is definitely legitimated. It expresses the ideal of a contemporary and instantaneous embrace of the infinite possible ways of creating meaning, all converging towards the abstract man as the only creator. In fact, in order that the polytheism of life forms can be possible, a reunification device is needed allowing the plurality to be traced back to a common poietic matrix: the universal man. "Reason" is the specific means for the jump into universalism, because it provides a first declination of instrumental neutrality, allowing the maximum poietic capacity. Reason, in fact, allows us to put away all the values and forms of life and, at the same time, to give them limitless citizenship.

In the juridical dimension, the decree of limitless accessibility translates in the passage from "government by men" to the "rule of law" (Bobbio, 1985), and therefore into the separation between law and justice: law is no longer an instrument aimed to realize specific goals or values, but it assumes a purely empowering function, regulating the smooth circulation of the life forms individually chosen (Barcellona, 1985, 1994). So, it becomes a mere reunification technique of a values' polytheism that, if not regulated, could lead to permanent conflict and the weaker to succumb. The rule is neutral and passive towards the players: the only concern is that everybody could make his own game, avoiding interaction to generate mutual obstacle. Atomization and reunification at the same time. The first tool of this institutional order is the modern "Constitution of liberty." It traces the basic frame of the collective and individual action spaces, regardless of the ends pursuable by freedom.

The imperative remains the guarantee of individual rights. Any restriction can be legitimized uniquely for reasons of fair coordination between them and cannot be justified by a preference reserved for one value to the detriment of another equivalent.

On the political side, the history of accessibility corresponds to the progression of the citizenship concept: civil, political, and social (Marshall, 1992). Civil citizenship (which substantially corresponds to what is defined by legal science as "the capacity to act," therefore to make a contract and to be bound by commitments, without unjustified limitations) and political citizenship (the right to elect our representatives at political assemblies and to be elected, that is to self-choose policies at every institutional level) are the original versions tied to the broader paradigm of liberal emancipation and the first translation of the instances of modernity. But this translation reveals to be unsuitable to ensure an effective opening of the accesses, if not for the benefit of restricted elites. The cause is, moreover, evident: this frame gives space only to "negative freedom," that is the freedom to desire what happens to us to desire. No space is given to "positive freedom." The first type ratifies the opportunities lying in the contingent reality, taking it as a matter of fact; the second kind of freedom works to overcome the given conditions in order to allow individuals acquiring capabilities to enjoy wider life chances (Veca, 1990). This results in an unparalleled system of limitless accessibility and circulation of values, meanings, projects, etc.

The mere formal granting of the "possibility" to realize his own life project is replaced by the public effort to create the preconditions for a real "empowering," extended, as far as possible, to the whole population. This option, which originally only belonged to a specific political area in Western countries (the social-democratic one), went soon to enrich the concept of citizenship with a new declination: "social citizenship." It represents a further step forward in the modern logic of liberation from all constraints and it probably challenges the most reluctant to abate: the scarcity of resources. Thus, social rights fully enter into the spectrum of modern states' fundamental rights, becoming a selection of universal minimum standards of security in the acquisition of vital resources, in the protection of the quality of life and work.

The historical realization (Hobsbawm, 1994) of this ideal framework allows Dahrendorf (1981) to maintain that modern societies have realized the principle "to give the maximum to the largest number" (p. 89). The social-democratic regime, as the most advanced and complete version of limitless accessibility, no longer belongs to a single party, but it leads all parties to share the aim of developing the three forms of citizenship (civil, political, social). Almost all governments, in fact, are informed by the same principles, only, their methods of application vary; we will almost always find policies aimed at limitless economic growth and at improving the living and working standards, a social policy based on the creation of equal chances for all (regardless of the disparity of the results), institutions modeled on the forms of classical democracy and a general political–cultural language framed by instrumentally rational action, as defined by Weber (1968). In this way, the political choice is solely exercised on the basis of concrete technical and administrative efficiency proven on the spot.

To sum up, in the growth regime, a public a-teleological power is installed, which never melds with the issue of what a good life is, because social life has to be considered as the unintentional result of the interaction between the single actors. They are sovereign in the elaboration and realization of their own life portion. The sole function of politics is to preserve or even cultivate the citizens' "biological" life, together with the administrative regulation of their free circulation (Foucault, 2001, 2011). So "growth" is nothing else than the result and the translation of the modern principle of institutional neutrality.

The nature of the "neutralitarian" institutional casing could be better understood through the interpretative lenses provided by Castoriadis (1975). Using these lenses, Mauro Magatti (2009) analyses how the institutionalization of social ties develops in modern democracies through the dialectic between two fundamental forms of meaning production: *legein* and *teukein*.

Modern man is originally characterized by the use of *legein* as main form of signification. *Legein* is the Greek verb that refers to the act of producing (the meaning of) the world by a conscious use of language. This is the mark that originally differentiates modernity from all the other eras. "Truth" is forged on the ground by *logos*. It doesn't rain from the top, i.e., from an extra-human authority coming from the sky or from the darkness of the tradition.

According to Castoriadis (1975), *legein* refers to the deployment of words, reasoning, argumentation, speech, and everything suitable to represent reality and interpret it as a whole, giving it sense. *Legein* means also linkage, connection, the search for relations between men, and between men and things (environment etc.), in order to infer an overall and consistent dynamics for a system as a whole. Democracy, hence, is the collective construction of sense.

However, the problem is that freedom in creating sense necessarily leads to a multiplication of possible visions: potentially, each individual carries his/her own sense. A modern, democratic human collective body could not shape itself sharing only one vision, because this shared vision will always be contestable, never adhering to the vision brought by each one.

The consequence of this problem is that in modernity, the *legein* is confined in a purely expressive, rhetorical, and intimate domain: everyone is free to express his/her unique vision, but no one can claim to implement it. This is a central paradox: modernity is the age in which everyone is encouraged to go out and search for "sense," but also everyone is prevented from translating it into a collective construction. So, the implementation of any political vision is structurally prevented by the primacy granted to individuals in defining and pursuing their own idea of "good." Under modernity, the recognition of micro-freedom becomes a veto to the great (collective) freedom.

Public authority is expected by definition to be neutral, passive in the face of the infinite variety of visions carried by each citizen. After all, none of these visions can be expected to be implemented by involving all the community, given that each one is assumed as carrying its own legitimate vision that necessarily clashes with that of others. A "neutralitarian regime" is generated to avoid this paradox of *legein*. In the name of autonomy, the main structural determinants of individual lives end up remaining totally untouched.

It is from this "neutralitarian regime" that the primacy of *teukein* springs. According to Magatti, the history of modernity is marked by the progressive decline of *legein*, in favor of *teukein* (2009).

Teukein refers to action, to the means for intervening over the world, pursuing goals which are useful to human welfare. It refers, in short, to technique. The development of the Promethean ability to do things, to act over the world, is another leitmotif of modernity, another form of signification, that moves parallel to that of *legein*. Given that *legein* can never be realized, *teukein* derives its legitimacy from the strength it demonstrates "on the ground," from the simple fact that one technique works better than another. If one technique increases men's capacity to do things, more than any other, it is to be accepted and espoused by all: because it enhances human autonomy and the opportunity to build the world in accordance with one's wishes. De facto, *teukein* takes the place of *legein* in building social life. Instead of a collective decision on how to shape the world, we simply adopt the technical system and its self-referential logic. It seems that neutrality improves individual autonomy and citizens empowerment. But clearly the structures that frame social life are not the output of a collective decision: they are the result of the technical development dynamics. *Teukein* rules the world, although the pretense is that it never affects the construction of sense in social life, as this in theory should be only the spontaneous result of the interaction between individuals, who are supposed to be sovereigns in devising and implementing their own life projects. The a–teleological character of democratic regime fosters the primacy of *teukein*.

Under these conditions, the aim of politics becomes the mere preservation of life: life for life's sake. Politics fosters the growth of the "organic" life of citizens (growth for growth's sake), together with the administrative control of their movements (Foucault, 1976). Life is preserved (or "grown") in order to allow the human beings to do everything they wish with it. Growth is then simply an expression of the modern principle of neutrality: it is 'rightly' indifferent to any human purpose, aiming only to increase the substantial opportunities of everyone to choose and achieve their own goals. In this sense, the principle of growth for growth's sake is equivalent to the principle of life for life's sake.

The outcomes of the growth regime

As we have seen, growth is not a "natural attitude" nor a simple "value," with an alleged miraculous appeal. Growth is the outcome of deep structural changes, giving birth to a characteristic institutional order, which in turn structurally requires growth for its reproduction. So, growth is the distillate of a specific social system. Any battle against the effects of growth cannot leave in the background the complex regime of which it is the fruit.

Now it's time to answer the second question asked above: why does the growth regime need to be rejected? To this aim we will rapidly review the main harmful outcomes of the growth regime in the economy and ecology, in institutions and politics, in the psychological and socio-anthropological dimension.

The Polanyian analysis of the effects of the self-regulating market remains unsurpassed. This exchange model leads neither more nor less to "the demolition of society" (Polanyi, 2001, p. 76). The reasons are to be recognized, in short, in the reduction of the factors of production to the state of "commodities," freely exchangeable like all others:

> But labor, land, and money are obviously not commodities.... Labor is only another name for human activity which goes with life itself, which in its turn is not produced for sale but for entirely different reasons, nor can that activity be detached from the rest of life, be stored or mobilized; land is only another name for nature, which is not produced by man; actual money, finally, is merely a token of purchasing power which, as a rule, is not produced at all, but comes into being through the mechanism of banking or state finance. None of them is produced for sale. The commodity description of labor, land and money is entirely factious.
>
> (Polanyi, 2001, pp. 75–76)

The marketization of the factors of production shows to be harmless for the social system. Society undertakes an irreversible process of disaggregation. In fact, the continuous value fluctuation of these founding elements of social cohesion, due to the blind dynamics of the law of supply and demand, becomes in the long run a harmful factor of uncertainty for social order.

> Labor and land are no other than the human beings themselves of which every society consists and the natural surroundings in which it exists. To

include them in the market mechanism means to subordinate the substance of society itself to the laws of the market.

(Polanyi, 2001, p. 75)

Labor cannot become a commodity like any other, because behind it there
are persons of flesh and bones with their families. When its prices and its
demands become variables depending on private bargaining, the existential
security of individuals is undermined, and the foundations of society are
weakened.

In the same way, if the value of money (i.e., of capital) begins to fluctuate
by virtue of the market *alea*, the income and the assets of social actors and
enterprises are subjected to a serious risk of depreciation. Also, this "commodity," whose functioning ultimately depends on an element of social
"trust," which is totally immaterial, cannot be left to the exchange between
individuals, but it needs a centralized administration that involves the whole
collectivity.

As well as the land: launching it on the "market," leaving it to free individual appropriation and exchange means jeopardizing biological collective
life. The delicate natural, environmental, and landscape balances could be
preserved only by interventions inspired by a complex and consistent
approach, which requires an integrated management at the communitarian
level. Without an informed and effective regulation in this field, the ecological order that ensures the survival of the species risks blowing up. The marketization of the factors of production is therefore an element of strong social
instability.

> To allow the market mechanism to be sole director of the fate of human
> beings and their natural environment indeed, even of the amount and use
> of purchasing power, would result in the demolition of society.... In dis-
> posing of a man's labor power the system would, incidentally, dispose of
> the physical, psychological, and moral entity "man" attaché to that tag....
> Nature would be reduced to its elements, neighborhoods and landscapes
> defiled, rivers polluted, military safety jeopardized, the power to produce
> food and raw materials destroyed. Finally, the market administration of
> purchasing power would periodically liquidate business enterprise, for
> shortages and surfeits of money would prove as disastrous to business as
> floods and droughts in primitive society.
>
> (Polanyi, 2001, p. 76)

To sum up, the entrusting of the management of these vertical pillars supporting social order to a horizontal device engenders economic and ecologic
disruptions.

At the political level, we witness the Bauman's paradox: the increase of
individual freedom coincides with the decrease of collective freedom
(Bauman, 1999). Any grand political project is structurally hampered by the

recognizing of individual autonomy in the definition and the pursuing of the idea of good.

The limitless accessibility regime provides a dream: modern man can now build the world according to his desires. But of the world, even of "my" little world, only an infinitesimal part can be controlled by me. The most powerful sources of determination are either invisible or out of anyone's control spectrum. I would be the domain of the collective sovereignty, but modern collective institutions, by statute (i.e., because of the neutralitarian regime), are disabled. Institutions are silent, faceless, transparent, neutral. They cannot carry out any autonomous project, since this would infringe the cardinal principle of individual autonomy, to whose support they must exclusively act. Collective autonomy, the only one able to intervene on the "context," on the general scenario that defines the coordinates within which any singular project can develop, is always abusive. The context must be nothing but the unintentional result of interactions between private actors. The institution does not have to interfere, except for regulating the circulation. This is not a democratic shortage, but, on the contrary, the physiological effect of the neutralitarian regime, which creates an intangible space (by the collective autonomy) for the individual. The recognizing of micro-freedom translates into a veto against macro-freedom, in the sense that collective freedom is subjected to the perpetual, structural veto, deriving from the logical primacy of the individual freedom. The great currents of determination of individual lives remain entirely untouched, paradoxically in the name of autonomy, but, above all, because of the stigma on sovereign power, the only entity able to contain private greed and to achieve broad objectives. Politics is abolished, in favor of an impolitic regime. The role of politicians aligns with that of building administrators, whose goal is to allow each apartment owner to enjoy his dwelling, ensuring that the common pertinences are well maintained. This results in the impression of an unchangeable world, where the forces that determine our lives are invisible and uncontrollable. Change is unthinkable. The great paradox is that on the one hand the limitless accessibility regime lures us with the promise of making everyone finally sovereign over everything, on the other, the "whole" becomes permanently intangible, accessing the original, unchangeable status of a datum, because of the structural defusing of collective sovereignty over the basic features of reality within which our unique poietic capacity is exercised.

It is what Baudrillard (2001, 2002) retranslates into the expression "universalist equivalence": every manifestation of (individual or collective) singularity that desperately aims at marking the context is immediately liquefied and reduced to a virtual preference among others, leaving the "system" untouched.

To sum up, limitless accessibility leads paradoxically to an unchangeable world. The promised pluriverse reduces to a fixed monoverse.

On the anthropological and psychosocial level, the consequences of the neutral growth regime are multiple and complex. In the first instance, we witness a sort of "anthropological deprivation," that is, the compression of some fundamental dimensions of the human being: the sociosymbolic dimension, the extrarational dimension and the reversive dimension.

The individualization process and the associated spasmodic search for autonomy lead the individual to progressively emancipate from any symbolic instance socially sanctioned. This does not imply a renunciation to the support, the warmth, the protection of the community, but a more traumatic loss of the actor's guidance codes. According to the authors that more explicitly radicalize the communitarian perspective, this move translates into an irremediable loss of meaning, very difficult to manage. The will for absolute transparency and for sovereignty over every dimension of life reveals the artificial character of any symbolic determination. Neither need nor the self-building of personal identity are sufficient to justify existence, which, in order to be legitimized, must always refer to the domains of the sacred, which is nothing more than the collective power itself (Durkheim, 1960).

The pervasiveness of the rational code – i.e., the specific means used by the individualized individual in order to put the twists of sociality and at the same time the internal driving instincts at a distance, for better calibrating his own conduct towards the linear pursuit of his chosen goals – ends up by rejecting emotions, the enchanted lands of affectivity, that is, the deepest dimensions of human life. It results in a dried and one-dimensional life, drained by the grayness of functional and standard intersections inside the anonymous social organization.

Finally, the new anthropological order rejects "reversion." We will broadly return to this point (guided by Bataille's work), since it is a fundamental junction in our argument. Summarizing, reversion evokes the unexplainable, counterintuitive human need to sometimes revert the unidirectional tension towards the desired things. This is inconceivable in the logic of the rational individual. More generally, it refers to the need to discard from the one-dimensional cage of the individual identity, aiming at emptiness and self-erasing.

But the main outcome of the neutralitarian regime on the anthropological side does not derive from the limitation factors considered up to now. It derives, on the contrary, from the trajectory of limitlessness (the "limitless accessibility" regime) triggered by modernity: we refer to what we've called the "anthropological stagflation" (Romano, 1993, 2008).

The new regime provides the individual with a multitude of access options (in a first "horizontal" phase, by leaving the elementary particles of society free to circulate and then, in the 20th century, by supporting them "vertically" with the strength of the State). Well, the paradox is that the options "inflation" coincides with the structural "devaluation" of each option (this is precisely "stagflation"), that inhibits the actor's desire to benefit from them. There is no hard substance in values: their attractiveness depends on the concrete circumstances that connote their apparition and their development process.

To better explain the effect, we can borrow from economics the law of diminishing marginal utility. As we know, it affirms the progressive decrease of the attitude of each additional dose of an asset to satisfy an individual need, until the utility of the single dose is reset, and the eventual following doses acquire a growing negative utility. Well, the regime of limitless accessibility has provided man with an extraordinary increase of commodities, options, life projects, opportunities to create sense and benefit from values. After the "blind" development of the 19th century (the age of the self-regulating market), during the 20th century, the State has distributed these opportunities to the largest number (by the continuous extension of citizenship rights). A general effect of diminishing marginal utility has attacked not only the goods, but also the value attached to the growing social chances. We witness a general evaporation of the values pursued by modern man: the value of the commodities that should satisfy his needs, the value of the material and symbolic entities which should fulfill his desires, the value of the self-elected ends, the value of the values framing his life path. This leads to a sort of "social paralysis," which we will discuss later. It precedes and prepares the economic saturation we are witnessing at the present time. It also explains the continuous amplification of the growth effort: due to the devaluation process, men are stimulated to produce more and more, in order to deceptively revive the values as stakes of social activation.

Another way to narrate this psychosocial drift was provided by Lacan with his "discourse of the capitalist" (Recalcati, 2010). In the initial times of capitalism, discipline and temperance were the main coordinates. Now capitalism fosters the rejection of any form of tie that hampers the free and maximum individual enjoyment. We precisely shift from "desire" to "enjoyment." The desire clashes against the Father and the Law and this dialectic development is the basis of the construction of personality. Nevertheless, enjoyment corresponds to immediate satisfaction, that in the long run atrophies the same ability of the subject to desire. Enjoyment is fulfilled inside the borders of individuality, without meeting the other (Recalcati, 2010).

For all these economic, ecological, political, anthropological, psychological, and social reasons the society of growth deserves to be overturned. But, to this purpose, it is necessary to take into account its complexity and the real nature of the growth obsession.

Notes

All translations in the book are by the author, unless otherwise indicated.
1 This is another element not well elucidated in the Riesmanian hypothesis: he does not give persuasive explanations about the reasons that have determined the increase in life expectancy.
2 This pretention justifies the Marxist denunciation of "false consciousness," which postulates the existence of an "ideal phantom of a not alienated conscience, or of an objective 'true' statute of the object: its use value" (Baudrillard, 1972, p. 97).

3 So the "good" is now easily recognizable, unambiguous, and transparent. It no longer depends on the different contexts: "a simple end replaces the sense multiplicity" (Baudrillard, 1972, p. 159).
4 "As useful values, all the goods are already comparable with each other, because they respond to the same functional/rational common denominator, to the same abstract injunction" (Baudrillard, 1972, p. 157).
5 "We believe in a real Subject, driven by needs and facing real objects and sources of satisfaction" (Baudrillard, 1972, p. 59).
6 "The individual is nothing more than the subject thought in the terms of the economy, re-thought, simplified and abstracted by economy" (Baudrillard, 1972, p. 159).
7 We have to consider that the distinction between analytic and normative dimension is often unlikely. It's an ideological way of depicting analytic work, in order to glorify it with the medals of neutrality and objectivity. If one thinks that in order to interpret social life we have to start "from the bottom," they will immediately be driven to promote political projects aimed at valuing grassroots. And vice versa.
8 He also finds out two balanced sums of both pure types: *idealistic and pseudo-ideational*.

9   The condition most favourable to the prosperity of agriculture exists when there are no entails, no unalienable endowments, no common lands, no right or redemption, no tithes or taxes or dues which punish industry, and levy a contribution upon agriculture, increasing in proportion to the expenses incurred, and the greater care paid to cultivation.

(Bentham, 1839, p. 68)

2 Degrowth

The rise of a radical alternative

For some years now, a thought has been emerging that explicitly and frontally promotes the exit from the growth regime, mainly denouncing its ecological unsustainability and, at the same time, striving for the realization of a degrowth society, i.e., a new social order freed from the goal, today still hegemonic, of unlimited economic growth and based on nonmaterialistic values.

Degrowth thought is rapidly spreading not only in academic departments and reviews (Kallis et al., 2010, 2012; Kallis, 2011; Cattaneo et al., 2012; Saed 2012; Sekulova et al., 2013; Whitehead, 2013; Kallis & Demaria, D'Alisa 2015; Weiss & Cattaneo, 2017; Cosme et al., 2017; Vandeventer et al., 2019), but also in antisystemic movements (Muraca, 2013): with Martinez-Alier et al. (2011), we can say that degrowth appears like an activist-led science (Demaria et al., 2013). It cannot be considered as a homogeneous and consistent sociopolitical theory. Beyond the great variety of approaches and cultural inspirations (D'Alisa et al., 2014), it is anyway difficult to find, in particular, an "analytical" side of the discourse, i.e., a specific way to read and understand social life and social action. The analytical approach is more often "implicit." So, when we consider degrowth thought, we primarily refer to its "critical" approach towards the current growth system and to the political solutions (including institutional and regulative frames) it suggests. "Degrowth signifies, first and foremost, a critique of the growth economy" (D'Alisa et al., 2014, p. 3). Therefore, the political battle undertaken by degrowthers is above all staged in the field of social imaginary: "it calls for the decolonization of public debate from the idiom of economism and for the abolishment of economic growth as a social objective" (D'Alisa et al., 2014, p. 3).

Degrowth gave birth to a bloated literature, considering its very young age in politics, culture, and science. Any attempt to draw an exhaustive review would therefore be incomplete. We will mention and synthesize here only its basic features, referring the reader to bibliography at the end of the book. The common ground, in fact, remains fairly consolidated, despite the multiple variations. We are not interested in designing a map of the traceable approaches, currents, and declinations. Rather, we will consider whether degrowth, in its basic consolidated structure, can challenge the growth-led regime, leading us towards a degrowth society.

The origins of degrowth

Degrowth, as we know it today, was born in France between 2000 and 2001 from radical eco-socialist milieus (Latouche, 2019). In Lyon, the first movement explicitly appealing to degrowth starts to promote the new keyword. The magazine *Casseur de Pub* (advertising breakers), founded by Clément, Cheynet, and Ghent is one of the first media outlets of the movement (D'Alisa et al., 2014). But maybe the most official foundational experience coincides with the conference "Défaire le développement, refaire le monde" ("Unpack Development, Rebuild the World") held at the UNESCO in Paris and organized by *La ligne d'horizon, association des amis de François Partant* (Berland et al., 2003). After some months, the magazine *La Décroissance* was founded. It will become a fundamental point of reference for anti-capitalists, pleading for a radical alternative. Then the movement spread to other Latin European countries. Anglo-Saxon countries followed, mainly thanks to the first international conference on degrowth held in Paris in 2008, under the impulse of Fabrice Flipo and François Schneider. Here the first degrowth manifesto was drafted (Research & Degrowth, 2010). Since then, the International Conference on Degrowth has occurred every two years, each time in a different location.

Indeed, the word already appeared in the scientific debate in 1994, thanks to the publication of the book *La Décroissance* a collection of essays by the founder of bioeconomics, Nicholas Georgescu-Roegen, edited by Ivo Rens and Jacques Grinevald (1994). Before that, the word degrowth had been used, maybe for the first time by André Gorz in 1972 in a debate organized by *Le Nouvel Observateur*. Then he advocated explicitly degrowth, always referring to the work of Georgescu-Roegen, in his book *Écologie et liberté* (Gorz, 1977; Leonardi, 2017).

But beyond the political and intellectual experiences that explicitly refer to the word, degrowth has been implicitly evoked by a different cultural matrix and, in particular, by several authors, who can be considered as precursors of this societal alternative (Gunderson, 2018). For many years, Serge Latouche (2016) has been carrying out a valuable work of reconstruction of the intellectual frame in which degrowth locates, leading a collection of small monographs, each one devoted to a degrowth precursor, in France (for the publisher Le passager clandestin) and in Italy (for the publisher Jaca Book).[1] Latouche identifies different categories of degrowth precursors: first of all we have to consider the premodern cultures, from the Greek philosophy (Diogene and Epicuro) to African, Amerindian, Asiatic wisdom; then some real pioneers like Fourier or Kropotkin; the great critics of the consumer society (Mumford, Bataille, Lanza del Vasto, Günther Anders, Georgescu-Roegen, Ellul, Panikkar, Bookchin, Ivan Illich, Castoriadis,

Partant, Baudrillard); the novelists like Tolstoy, Tagore, Huxley, Orwell, Pasolini, Terzani; the politicians (Gandhi, Berlinguer, Langer); and finally the "undatables," i.e., those who, although alluding to a society freed from obsession with growth, have however married antidemocratic, or even fascist ideological and political paths.

Anyway, we will here focus on the school of thought that perhaps more than others in recent times has provided the most systematic and consistent intellectual framework or cultural *humus* for the degrowth alternative (beyond the original intentions). We refer to "anti-utilitarianism," of which Serge Latouche (probably the most important founder of degrowth thinking) has been one of the protagonists.

Anti-utilitarianism is a school of thought that critiques the hegemony of the epistemological postulates of economics in the humanities and social sciences. Anti-utilitarians assert the crucial importance of the social bond when compared to self-interest. They outline a gift–exchange paradigm that aims at overstepping two major frameworks of the social sciences: holism and methodological individualism.

In 1981, the French sociologist, Alain Caillé, and the Swiss anthropologist, Gérald Berthoud, gave birth to MAUSS – Mouvement anti-utilitariste dans les sciences sociales (Anti-utilitarian Movement in the Social Sciences).[2] This brilliant acronym reproduces the surname of the author of *The Gift* (1924), Marcel Mauss. Mauss together with Karl Polanyi inspired the work of the group.

The movement was led from the beginning by Alain Caillé and gathered intellectuals from different fields of knowledge: Serge Latouche, economist and philosopher (one of the fathers of the degrowth alternative), Ahmet Insel (economist and political scientist), Jean-Luc Boilleau (sociologist and philosopher), Jacques Godbout (anthropologist), Philippe Rospabé (economist and anthropologist). They first created the *Bulletin du Mauss* and, in 1988, the *Revue du Mauss*, printed by the prestigious French publisher *La Découverte* (initially quarterly and, since 1993, half-yearly).

MAUSS is today configured as a large network of researchers located in Europe, North America, North Africa, and the Middle East. It is characterized by a wide variety of approaches, subjects, and application fields. Its main theoretical aim is to establish a new epistemological basis for universalism and democracy. This effort – more systematic and accomplished in the works of Alain Caillé – has developed around three main reflection axes: the individual, the social bond, and politics.

Anti-utilitarians challenge the theoretical approaches that interpret any human action as departing from the pivotal axis of the "individual" and thus oriented towards self-satisfaction:

> we qualify as utilitarian any doctrine based on the claim that human subjects are governed by the logic of selfish calculation of pleasures and pains, by their interest only, or by their preferences only; and that this is

good because there is no other possible foundation of ethical norms other than the law of happiness for individuals and their communities.

(Caillé, 1989, p. 13)

The object of criticism of anti–utilitarians is an ideological matrix that cuts across thought and the wider culture:

utilitarianism is not a philosophical system or a component among others of the dominant ideology in modern societies. Rather it has become that same ideology; to the point that, for modern people, it is largely incomprehensible and unacceptable what cannot be translated in terms of usefulness and instrumental effectiveness.

(Caillé, 1989, pp. 4–5)

Anti–utilitarians criticize utilitarianism because it reduces the human being. The battle to be waged, they claim, should insist on the recognition of the complexity and the plurality of forms of life. Anti–utilitarianism, far from qualifying itself as anti–modern thought, aims at rediscovering the true meaning of modernity, restoring the scientific spirit against scientism, reason against rationalism, democracy against technocracy. Caillé resumes, in this sense, the Brahmanic classification of man's goals (puruṣārtha): pleasure (*kama*), interest (*artha*), duty (*dharma*), and dissipative liberation from all aims (*moksha*) (1989, pp. 89ff.). According to Caillé, utilitarianism has reduced a multiplicity of goals into the sole kingdom of *artha*. But he also criticizes other schools of thought that translate the ontological multiplicity into one of the three sacrificed motives: the Freudian school devoted to the *kama*, the holistic school pointing to *dharma*, or the existentialist mood (à la Bataille) in search of *moksa*. The counter-project proposed by anti–utilitarians is a contemporary citizenship to all Brahmanic levels of existence, i.e., to all "multiple states of the subject." This claim is articulated on both an analytical level (the multi-teleology of the human being has an ontological connotation) and, as we shall see later, on a political level.

The second pole of reflection, the social bond, coincides with the reevaluation of gift logic. According to Mauss, the gift is here understood as a "total social fact." Just like the "underlying unconscious structure" envisioned by Lévi-Strauss, the gift becomes the archetypal performer or the universal symbolic matrix of the alliance between individuals and groups. It acts on a micro-sociological level by the device of the triple obligation – "to give, to receive and to return" – but it can be extended to the meso-sociological scale of the "association" and, finally, to "Politics," i.e., the macro-sociological frame. "Each one of these three terms – gift, association and politics – is a metaphor, a symbol and a tool for interpreting the others" (Caillé, 1998, p. 236).

In the second half of the 1990s, the political inclination of the movement accentuated, starting from the "thirty theses for a new and universalist left" (discussed in various issues of the *Revue du Mauss*, starting from 9(1), 1997). On the political side, anti-utilitarianism identifies with the project of "democracy for democracy": the democratic ideal can be revitalized only by doing away with any aims or interests, especially egotistic, from the collective discussion. According to Caillé, the main obstacle to democracy, and the main reason for the decline of politics, is a lack of alternative social life patterns so that, for instance, even discussion or selection of said preferences is precluded by the utilitarian ideology, leading to depoliticization. Democracy must enhance diversity by offering a variety of lifestyles, increase public space for discussion, and pluralize the possibilities of self-realization. One key proposal in this direction is the basic income, but "radically unconditional." It is necessary to decouple income from specific social benefits, as this coupling limits the freedom of citizens to experience the irreducible plurality of human aims. Instead, the largest number of citizens possible should have the chance to realize themselves, and to express who they are and what they want to be. Anti-utilitarians call for a "political" critique of boundlessness and excess (Dzimira, 2007). They advocate a political project that metabolizes the principles of "reversibility" – against the externalities of progress that threaten collective existence – and of "reciprocity," against the power of most developed societies, which limits and threatens the chances for life and action of less developed societies and future generations (Caillé, 2006).

Thanks to Serge Latouche, the so-called anti-pope of MAUSS (given his differences with Caillé) the anti-utilitarian movement produced one of the main strands of degrowth. Latouche (2001) is less indulgent towards Western capitalism, which he approaches mainly through the lens of criticism of development. While Caillé aims to restore the 'true' meaning of modernity against its perversions, Latouche pleads for a radical rethinking of modernity, in order to cut off its genetic link with utilitarianism. This path leads to degrowth.

The criticism of growth: ecological and social unsustainability

Beyond the recent economic crisis (started in 2008), the dominant regime – degrowthers claim – produces a much more worrying "ecological" and "social" crisis (Mylondo, 2009; D'Alisa et al., 2014, pp. 6–15).

> growth is uneconomic and unjust, it is ecologically unsustainable and it will never be enough. Moreover, growth is likely to be coming to an end as it encounters external and internal limits.
>
> (D'Alisa et al., 2014, p. 6)

The internal limits refer first of all to the fact that growth is an autophagic machine. Technological innovation cannot be unlimited (Gordon, 2012). Saturation of social demand is always lurking, so it is always more difficult to find market outlet for the growing commodities, assuring a constant profit level (Piketty & Goldhammer, 2014). The marginal returns on investment in money and in organizational complexity diminish constantly (Tainter, 2003; Bonaiuti, 2014).

But the external limits are even more worrying. For Latouche the growth regime has to be stigmatized because it jeopardizes life itself: "a radical change is an absolute necessity ... to avoid a brutal and tragic catastrophe" (2007, p. 10). We have to reverse this regime in order to preserve the survival chances of Planet Earth and its inhabitant (Jackson, 2008; Anderson & Bows, 2011; Victor, 2012; Perkins, 2019):

> With continuous global growth most planet ecosystem boundaries will be surpassed. There is a strong and direct correlation between GDP and the carbon emissions that change the climate. Global carbon intensity (C/$) by 2050 should be 20–130 times lower than today, when the reduction from 1980 to 2007 was just 23 per cent.
>
> (D'Alisa et al., 2014, p. 7)

Considering that, as a rule, human activity transforms energy and materials of low entropy in waste and pollution with high entropy (Georgescu-Roegen, 1971, 2014), a regime of unlimited growth becomes incompatible with the available nonrenewable resources, with the regeneration speed of the biosphere and of renewable resources (Bonaiuti, 2011).

Many trust in "dematerialization" of the economy and technological progress (going towards cleaner solutions) to reduce the impact on environmental balance. But, normally efficiency, while reducing risks and costs, makes resources more affordable, so it ends up boosting consumption and thus putting a strain on the carrying capacity of the planet (Inglehart, 1990, 1997). This is what the Jevons's paradox tells us.

Furthermore, dematerialization via the "service economy" is often an illusionism, because it is only the tip of the iceberg, i.e., the final form of a heavy process that embodies a big amount of materials and energy (Odum & Odum, 2001; Schneider, 2008).

Moreover, pollution and waste are mainly poured into the peripheries of the world, engendering environmental injustice (Carmin & Agyeman, 2011; Rodríguez-Labajos et al., 2019; Singh, 2019).

"Social" unsustainability then adds to ecological unsustainability (Kallis, Schneider, & Martinez-Alier, 2010). First, the alleged well-being produced by the growth regime is "unmasked" as the fruit of illusionism. If from GDP – as it must be done – we deduct noxious products directly linked to the externalities of growth (costs of pollution, healthcare, prisons, etc.) we will discover its negative progression in all Western countries over the last decades (Matthey, 2010).

In general, growth ideology assumes a direct correlation between an increase in GDP and collective happiness. According to degrowthers, on the contrary, there is an explicit inverse correlation between well-being and material wealth. The pursuit of personal richness determines the degradation of social environment; thus, the increase of well-having will always lead to a decrease of well-being. The GDP growth, Latouche warns us, produces unhappiness and weakens social relations. Well-having decreases well-being.

> Growth is uneconomic because, at least in developed economies, "illth" increases faster than wealth. The costs of growth include bad psychological health, long working hours, congestion and pollution. GDP counts costs, such as the building of a prison or the clean-up of a river, as benefits. As a result, GDP may still increase, but in most developed economies welfare indicators such as the Genuine Progress Index or the Index of Sustainable Economic Welfare have stagnated after the 1970s. Above a certain level of national income, it is equality and not growth that improves social well-being.
>
> (D'Alisa et al., 2014, p. 6)

In fact, as the ecological economists have shown, beyond a certain threshold the GDP growth starts to increase much more than wealth (Daly, 1996). Kubiszewski et al. (2013), by collecting data from 17 countries in the period 1950–2003, assert that beyond US$7,000 of GDP/capita the GPI/capita – i.e., the Genuine Progress Indicator (Daly & Cobb, 1989), which takes into account the depreciation of community capital in the calculation of the welfare produced by economic activity – does not increase anymore. At that point, social welfare could only be improved by equality and not by growth (Wilkinson & Pickett, 2009). On the contrary, growth tends to increase inequalities and social injustice. And this is also due to the "social limits to growth" (Hirsch, 1978). Moreover, the general process of commodification (Gómez-Baggethun, 2014) promoted by growth implies the constant erosion of the precious nonutilitarian dimensions of the human being (Caillé, 1989).

> Care, hospitality, love, public duty, nature conservation, spiritual contemplation; traditionally, these relations or 'services' did not obey a logic of personal profit. Nowadays they increasingly become objects of market exchange, valued and paid for in the formal GDP economy. Profit motivations crowd out moral or altruistic behaviours and social wellbeing diminishes as a result.
>
> (D'Alisa et al., 2015, p. 6)

Outline of a degrowth society

Normally, ecological economists interpret degrowth, first and foremost, as a form of downscaling of production and consumption, equal for all, in order to reduce the withdrawal of energy and material resources (Kallis, Kerschner, & Martinez-Alier, 2012; Kallis, 2013; Sorman & Giampietro, 2013; Alexander & Yacoumis, 2018; Schröder et al., 2019).

Degrowth signifies a society with a smaller metabolism, but more importantly, a society with a metabolism which has a different structure and serves new functions.

Degrowth does not call for doing less of the same. The objective is not to make an elephant leaner, but to turn an elephant into a snail.

(D'Alisa et al., 2015, p. 4)

But against the ecological and social drifts of the growth regime, degrowthers do not simply suggest a deliberate decrease of GDP (Borowy & Schmelzer, 2017; Cassiers et al., 2017).

Degrowth is neither *another* growth, nor *another* development (sustainable, social, solidaristic, etc.), but the construction of another society, a society of frugal abundance, a "post-growth" society or a form of prosperity without growth (Jackson, 2010). In other words, it is not immediately an economic project, another economy, but a societal project that implies an exit from economy as an imperialist reality and discourse.

(Latouche, 2019, pp. 7–8)

Degrowth has to be mainly intended as *a*-growth, i.e., the liberation from the productivist obsession, in order to rediscover other human dimensions, first and foremost the relational one (Schneider et al., 2010; Andreoni & Galmarini, 2013).

Degrowth signifies also a desired direction, one in which societies will use fewer natural resources and will organize and live differently than today. "Sharing," "simplicity," "conviviality," "care," and the "commons" are primary significations of what this society might look like.

Degrowth is not the same as negative GDP growth. Still, a reduction of GDP, as currently counted, is a likely outcome of actions promoted in the name of degrowth. A green, caring and communal economy is likely to secure the good life, but unlikely to increase gross domestic activity.

(D'Alisa et al., 2014, pp. 3–4)

The aim is not to set up a society based on deprivation and scarcity, in order to preserve the systemic balance of the planet as much as possible. Instead, the idea is to recover, thanks to a moderation in the material dimension, a more convivial, human-friendly way of life (Jackson, 2016; Rosa & Henning, 2017): "a degrowth transition is not a sustained trajectory of descent, but a transition to convivial societies who live simply, in common and with less" (D'Alisa et al., 2014, p. 11).

Latouche explains this point of view very effectively and evocatively:

It is a question of ... striving for a better quality of life and not for an unlimited growth of the GDP.

(2007, p. 62)

It is necessary to separate the improvement of individual conditions and the quantitative growth of material production. In other words, we need to decrease "well-having," measured by economic indicators, and to improve really lived "well-being."

(Latouche, 2007, p. 98)

happiness comes from living well, not from living long.

(Latouche, 2007, p. 117)

As often happens with great utopias (see for example Marxism), it is difficult to find in the existing literature a clear design of what a degrowth society should be. Few have ventured into the construction of an alternative social model, inspired by the principles implied in the critique to growth-led society (see Kallis, 2018a, 2018b). It is difficult to find an illustration of the social regulation criteria and of the ordinary functioning of a degrowth society. One of the best-known and advanced attempts in this direction is the "eight Rs" program suggested by Serge Latouche.[3] It is designed around eight keywords (eight verbs) from which it is possible to imagine and to implement a new social order: reconceptualizing, reevaluating, restructuring, redistributing, reducing, reusing, recycling, to relocalizing.

First, we have to rethink our current words whose meanings are often ossified by use and by cultural hegemony (Pörksen, 1995). Poverty and richness, scarcity and abundance, "value," etc. are complex concepts whose very content is defined from time to time by the forges of public opinion. Taking them for granted, we participate – often unconsciously and accidentally – in the consolidation of the growth-led regime. So, first, we have to "reconceptualize," for example, what to be "rich" really means. This is not obvious. In our societies, we tend to immediately identify the term with material wealth. In a society of degrowth, on the contrary, it will refer to a relational diversity and plenitude. Poverty, at the same time, is not necessarily hell. It could evoke a condition of soberness, where the compulsion to consume more and more is replaced by caring people and the environment around us (Rahnema, 2004). Therefore, we always need to question ourselves rationally and critically on the meaning of words and concepts we currently use: this is the first step in constructing a degrowth alternative.

Reevaluating means completely rethinking the set of values that frame our lives. The current key themes are more or less selfishness, competition, working hard, consuming hard, globalism, heteronomy, efficiency, and rationalism. Degrowthers oppose this list with a completely reversed one: altruism, cooperation, promoting good living (work–life balance), sociability, localism, autonomy, beauty, and reasonableness. By following these key themes, we would be led to another world, where the compulsion to growth is completely erased.

The new set of values will drive the "restructuring," the adaptation, and the conversion of our social patterns: economic structures (what, how, and how much to produce), consumption models, lifestyles, etc. The grids supporting these activities have to be shaped in order to better meet the new social goals. Work organization, for example, would no longer aim at maximizing efficiency and the quantity of manufactured goods, but would have to satisfy workers' needs to enjoy their work, to rediscover its social value and its role in mediating the relation between subject and object.

Redistributing means avoiding the individual grab of the planet's resources, ensuring at the same time that every human being can access, on an equal basis (with respect both to his contemporaries and to future generations), a share of the available wealth sufficient to provide him with a dignified living, without destroying the environmental balances and the reserves of nonrenewable resources.

It is then necessary to "reduce," first and foremost the unuseful and harmful activities and forms of production. In this sense, GDP is a very unreliable wealth indicator, because it sums up in a single bill everything that is produced in a given territorial unity regardless of their real contribution to collective happiness or wellbeing (Garcia et al., 2018; Büchs & Koch, 2019). Whether they are flowers or weapons, hospitals or prisons, it doesn't matter. The construction of a new prison, in fact, is an indicator of bad collective integration, but GDP registers it as a very positive item. The sale of new cars will generate more pollution, which means more respiratory disease, which in turn will increase healthcare expenses, etc. At each step, GDP will report an increase, despite the multiplication of social damages. So, first, it is necessary to reduce useless and harmful productions.

Anyway, it is necessary to bring back production and consumption within environmental limits. In this sense, the "ecological footprint" is a useful tool. It translates in terms of land availability, the natural resources required to sustain a given individual or collective lifestyle. It tells us that if all inhabitants were to acquire the living standards of the average US citizen, we would need several planets to provide the required natural resources. But, at the moment, only one planet is available.

Last, but not least, we have to reduce the working time, both for redistributing the amount of available work (increasingly reduced due to technology), thus giving everyone the chance to earn a living and get out of productivism.

"Reusing" means, first and foremost, extending life cycle of commodities against their programmed obsolescence imposed by corporations, in order to limit the consumption of natural resources. It is necessary to always try to repair the tools, items, and commodities of our daily life. This pattern naturally merges into recycling practices aimed at recovering the nonrecyclable waste of our activities and at revalorizing the decomposable waste within a zero-waste strategy.

Reducing, reusing, and recycling lead us to one of the cornerstones of the degrowth society: the principle of stationarity. The idea is to interrupt the dynamics of unlimited growth, reaching constant levels of production that ensure the reproducibility of renewable resources and reduce the exploitation of nonrenewable resources to a minimum.

In this regard, Latouche properly rejects the theories (often coming from leftist intellectuals) that depict the steady state as a result of the spontaneous dynamics of capitalism (Daly, 1996; Harvey, 2005, 2006, 2011). On the contrary, he supports the need for a radical and deliberate political change towards this goal, inspired by the wisdom of traditional, premodern societies (Lauriola, 2013). If we acknowledge that "our survival requires a reconstruction of a harmonious relationship with nature,"[4] then we have to remember that:

> up to the eighteenth century, all human societies have worked according to a sustainable reproduction pattern....[5] The vernacular society is sustainable because it has adapted its ways of life to the natural environment.[6]

The last keyword has important implications for the institutional framework of degrowth. Relocalizing means, first and foremost: "producing locally most of the goods required to satisfy the population's needs, starting from local firms financed by locally collected savings" (Latouche, 2007, p. 133).

But re-localizing does not only concern the economic field. It also includes the "local political utopia." For degrowthers, in general, the local dimension is not only a space for the reconstruction of social ties and lost DIY ("do it yourself") production practices; it is the main "institutional" container and the preferable scale of application of the degrowth alternative. Latouche, for example, retrieves the "bioregion" concept of Panikkar (1995): a "homogeneous" territorial entity, where biophysical elements (plants, animals, water, etc.) are linked to the history of people in a harmonious embrace. The geographical extent of such bioregions is open, ranging from the "small district republic" to the municipality or the inter-district. Anyway, Latouche states, it should not exceed the threshold of 30,000 inhabitants, beyond which the specter of alienating depersonalization that now poisons the growth society will return. For degrowth advocates, the local dimension provides two conditions without which a democracy is unmanageable and deprived of any sense: the personalization of citizens' relations (it is the idea of "grassroots democracy" developed by Fotopoulos, 1997) and the embedding of institutions within a specific cultural context, achievable only at a local scale. Of course, the proposed bio-units are not supposed to be closed, autistic monads, but connected to one another within bottom-up confederations. The supposed result would be a democratic pluri-verse of cultures.

Images of the transition

How do degrowth advocates see the transition to a degrowth society? How to take people out of the hegemony of the growth regime? Which is the path that leads to the new horizon? How to politically struggle for the advent of a society of degrowth?

The debate on this topic is more developed in the activists' milieus than in the scientific literature. Normally, the contrast between "voluntary" and "involuntary" degrowth is considered as relevant (Bonaiuti, 2018).[7] Involuntary degrowth — mostly widespread in the Anglo-Saxon world — promotes

> a view of the future that the production economy will contract anyway, whether we like it or not ... so that the task of the degrowth movement is to prepare for, and ameliorate, that contraction as best as we can.
>
> (Davey, 2014)

Voluntary degrowth instead prevails in the "continental" versions of the project (Latouche, 2007, 2014; Deriu, 2014). Here degrowth does not appear as "an adaptation to inevitable limits, but a desirable project to be pursued in the search for autonomy (i.e., to decide the future in common freed from external imperatives and givens)" (D'Alisa et al., 2104, p. 8).

But the distinction between the two approaches is not so relevant if we consider their political outcome. Despite the different starting point, both converge towards "voluntary simplicity" (Alexander, 2013; Alexander & Gleeson, 2018). Change is imagined as the promotion here and now of anti-growth "values" by staging social alternatives from the grassroots and radicalizing their horizontal form. So, in the voluntary simplicity strategy, "agency" is the privileged dimension (Boonstra & Joosse, 2013): activists secede from the public arena where the majority of people lie, in order to build a small world together with those who only share the same values and visions.

> A degrowth or steady-state economy will depend for its realization on the emergence of a post-consumerist culture, one that understands and embraces 'sufficiency' in consumption.
>
> (Alexander, 2013, p. 300)

Obeying this path, an elite, most "aware" of the necessity of degrowth, will set a good example, staging degrowth practices, here and now, without waiting to "take the power." Degrowthers promote collective and personal experiences of simplicity; they engage in voluntary simplicity circles, found small degrowth or other eco-communities (Xue, 2014), transition towns, nowtopias, back-to-landers etc. (Cacciari, 2011, 2018; Demaria et al., 2013; D'Alisa et al., 2014; Nelson & Schneider, 2018). All done in the hope that their practical virtues will stand out so obviously and infect the rest of the citizens. This kind of action is not political in the traditional sense of the term. Degrowthers do not call for storming the Winter Palace (the institutions). Faithful to a horizontal logic, they act immediately in the social sphere, giving concrete proof of the feasibility of a degrowth alternative.

At the basis of this approach there is a strong distrust towards politics, intermediate social bodies, power and institutions, which has its deep roots in the post-1968 cultural climate (Illich, 1972, 1977; Boltanski & Chiapello, 2007; Heikkurinen et al., 2019), to which we will return in the last chapter. This trait is well documented by Cornelius Castoriadis (2005): "social change is not the outcome of laws and decrees, and even less of terror, family, language, religion" (p. 178). It is considered as something immanent to the human being, which in due course manifests itself spontaneously without external stimuli or injunctions. So, the affair concerns only the individuals:

> the transformation takes place only with self-transformation and all attempts to radically change the ways of thinking and lifestyles by coercion have produced terrible results, as the experience of the Red Khmers in Cambodia showed.
>
> (Latouche, 2007, p. 109)

Evidently, if change is the fruit of a self-transformation there is no need to undertake conflict actions, or simply a political struggle for hegemony. We only have to wait for the epiphany of change. At most, it's enough to set an example, staging virtuous practices that will be acknowledged and imitated by the wider audience, due to their objective validity.

It is true that this general pattern of pseudo-political action applies less on the part of the degrowth movement that approaches degrowth from an environmental conflict perspective (Martinez-Alier, 2002; Martinez-Alier et al., 2010; D'Alisa et al., 2013), and which has as its starting point the social conflicts and movements against development projects carried on by public entities or private companies. Anyway, consistently with the goal of relocalizing, political action is more often staged in the local arena. As Yves Cochet (2005) suggests:

> We must play an active role in municipal life ... promoting practices and cultures of sobriety: more pedestrian areas and cycle paths instead of motorways, more small shops instead of large malls and shopping centers, smaller buildings instead of big buildings and towers, more proximity and personal services, less urban zoning.
>
> (p. 200)

The underlying trust is that a specific political–territorial frame (the "localist" one) necessarily generates and reproduces a specific political agenda: once a local community is democratized and autonomous, it will spontaneously choose the "good" values of sobriety, measure, "small is beautiful," etc. (Magnaghi, 2010).

Growth and degrowth: two sides of the same pattern?

> Whoever tries to keep their life will lose it, and whoever loses their life will preserve it
>
> (Luke 17:33)

The bourgeois ethics aims at eliminating death in all its forms while imposing life itself as a value.... The exaltation of biological life as a supreme value is inhuman and destroys the very meaning of existence in its thickness quality. The West, making the world disenchanted, makes terrestrial life the value par excellence.

(Serge Latouche)

Can the degrowth project, as it is currently set, aspire to defuse and reverse the growth regime? Can it really aim to change this world, transforming current systemic logics and promoting a social alternative freed from the compulsion to grow?

Our answer is: no. For at least two reasons. First, the strategy designed for the transition to degrowth society is ineffective (we will return to this in the last chapter). But the decisive reason is that the degrowth project, in its current formulation, does not represent, looking at it in depth, a real alternative to the regulation pattern, the anthropological stakes, and the value system of the growth regime. From multiple points of view, it proves to be compatible with the growth regime and, in some ways, it participates in its consolidation.

Far from helping to free our societies from the obsessive utilitarian logic, degrowth contributes, in many ways, to reconfirm a political anthropology unequivocally marked by utilitarianism.

It is not a nominalistic concern. Claiming to tear away from degrowth the anti-utilitarian seal may appear a sterile academic exercise. Indeed, it is the first step in order to radically rethink its epistemological foundations and its political translation, since we ardently support the project of a degrowth society, but we are at the same time persuaded that its premises and contents condemn it to an ephemeral, illusory success, although potentially wide, leaving its horizon of meanings substantially unattainable.

Anti-utilitarians in fact blame degrowthers for the choice of the keyword "degrowth," since everything is dipped in economic fetishism (although in an inverted form). All alternatives inspired by degrowth entail, in the end, a sober lifestyle and economic restraint (so, similar to the ethical discipline that characterizes Western capitalism, as Weber first noted). But these polemical arguments are insufficient and not well formulated. Latouche, moreover, has been able to convincingly reply: first, to make a breakthrough in a society largely dominated by the "enemy," it is necessary, at least in the first instance, to share its vocabulary if we want our voice to be heard by a wide audience; second, the goal is not to achieve negative growth, a deliberate reduction of the goods produced, but to build a society freed from the myth of growth (2007, 2019). The aim is more properly "a-growth" rather than degrowth. But obviously the word "a-growth" would not make for a catchy slogan.

The homogeneity of degrowth to the regime it aims to break down is more solid and goes well beyond the alleged inappropriateness of the adopted slogan. Besides, it is the same anti-utilitarian background that reveals a cultural homogeneity to utilitarianism. And precisely from this point it is necessary to start.

Utilitarianism inside anti-utilitarianism

Beyond the interpretative categories devised or supported by the MAUSS, the continuity between the growth regime and anti-utilitarian thought emerges above all in the sociopolitical project stemming, more or less explicitly, from anti-utilitarian reflection, from its basic features and their implications in the present world, as well as from its posture towards the sociopolitical project it aims to oppose (i.e., the utilitarian one).

No anti-utilitarian project is conceivable unless it starts from the opposition to what we have called the logic of limitless accessibility. This challenge, in turn, is possible only if the ultimate absence of substance inside any meaning and value is admitted: it is not viable, in fact, if we continue to believe in the self-consistency of the human being, ethically worthy to be revealed. Economism, individualism, utilitarianism, etc., do not operate for the suppression and the reduction of human beings, but in order to neutrally enable them to always produce meaning. These intellectual tools are not responsible for the ossification of the human being. Human beings are exclusively the victims of their own inconsistency.

This awareness does not generally belong to anti-utilitarians. The criticism of utilitarianism is very telling. As we have seen, in fact, anti-utilitarians blame utilitarianism for its alleged reductive conception of human existence. Therefore, the battle to be carried out mainly consists of the acknowledgment of the complexity and the plurality of life forms, hence of further accessibility. In this sense, anti-utilitarianism does not mark a discontinuity with respect to other modern and liberal mainstream sociopolitical theories, like those of Popper, Habermas, the postmodernists, the multiculturalists. The restoring of the scientific spirit against scientism, reason against rationalism, democracy against technocracy can be translated, in general, as the will to defend the alleged good modernity of the origins against the present bad modernity, believing that the latter is nothing but a putsch realized by nefarious "utilitarianism."

The claim against the reduction of human ends at the domain of "artha" (the interest) actually results in the request of a hyper-limitless accessibility, which is declined both on the analytical level (the human multi-finalism as an ontological character) and on the sociopolitical level, by, specifically, the project of "democracy for democracy" (i.e., not subordinated to the selfish aims of individuals).

We have to ask whether the pursuit of the limitless "manifestation of what a person is and what he wants to be" is not consubstantial with the limitless increase of the wish to have, which corresponds to the logic of unlimited growth (one of the main fronts of anti-utilitarian criticism). After all, growth is nothing but the prosaic, trivial, neutral, historical, and stylized translation of the drive to limitless self-manifestation. Having more multiplies my chances to be what I want to be. In this sense, economism and individualism can be interpreted as inventions having the same purpose of the democratic invention. The autonomization of development, the fact that it becomes an end in itself, is not imputable to utilitarianism, but to the vanishing constitution of the human being, who evaporates when solicited to self-manifest. For this reason, the attempt to recover the original sense of development (empowering the human being) risks leading to human ossification. It is the limitlessness logic that leads reason to rationalism, science to scientism, and democracy to technocracy, not the reductive hand of utilitarianism.

"Democracy for democracy" represents one of the most consistent translations of the modern principle of neutrality, i.e., the tension towards an anonymous, faceless, disembodied social construction set up by modern liberal thinkers (Rawls, 1999; Wolfe, 2001; Mill, 2005; von Hayek, 2006; Rodotà 2012). The imperative is to clear the field of any specific meaning. Paradoxically, utilitarianism is criticized just in the name of this principle (in fact, utility evokes – only one – possible moral way, coinciding with the growth of pleasure and the minimization of pain) and not, as one would expect, for its destructive effect on the sense of life. The "neutralitarian" strategy is reconfirmed and it reaches its peak when Caillé calls for choosing by a lottery at every level the political representatives: here, the exaltation of humanistic abstraction coincides with the radical distrust towards real men.

"Radically unconditional" basic income (Caillé, 1989, p. 115) is a further variation of neutrality. It is a disembodied device, which binds the activity of meaning creation to an amount of money, as a universal equivalent. This is an implicit legitimation of the strategy always adopted by utilitarianism and economism: the quantitative fetishism as a means for neutrally enabling individuals to think and realize their own life project.

Also, the application of the gift paradigm to the social bond theory raises some concerns (Caillé, 1998). The argumentative ways by which Caillé legitimizes the translation of the gift archetypal micro-social dimension into "association" and then into the political dimension refer to an unsatisfactory quantitative–spatial criterion. First, a temporal hiatus lies among the practices we have considered. Then, as we will see later with Bataille, he completely erases the sense of reversion and loss included in the gift logic. "Association" and "Politics" are historically characterized by the "projective logic" (Maffesoli, 1998) typical of modernity; the gift logic, instead, always implies a certain degree of heteronomy, hierarchy, a-finalism, dissipation, and it is continually eaten up by the worm of unawareness (Latouche, 1997, p. 65). Caillé sanitizes the gift to recycle it as the foundation of the edifying and voluntarist logic of "association" and "politics." The gift is co-opted at the service of the finalistic projectivism, it is suggested as a new universal lubricant of the exhausted paradigm of modernity.

Maffesoli shows that the political–associationist projective sociality has nothing to share with the tribal–communitarian form of aggregation (Maffesoli, 1998). They are two paradigms that respond to different logics and needs, completely irreconcilable. They can add up (as often happens in the new business realities, mainly those who are digitally led) respecting each other's specificities, but not merging into one another.

The miracle of the fusion of *Gemeinschaft* (community) and *Gesellschaft* (society) has no evidence in the empirical reality (Tönnies, 1963). We can avoid sacrificing personalization on the altar of functional tension only if we definitively anesthetize it: as is the case for the third sector.

In this sense, anti-utilitarianism lends itself to easy instrumentalizations: the World Bank, the IMF, governmental agencies, and NGOs for international cooperation everywhere in the world (mainly in developing countries) promote the dissemination of associations and intermediate bodies, etc. as a lintel of market and liberal–democratic institutions, that is, of the growth society. If "association" and the "political" are proposed as natural extensions of the universal matrix of gift (dwelling at the basis of the social bond), then it becomes possible, legitimate, and worthy to export them universally. Anti-utilitarians, beyond their intentions, serve the reproduction of the growth society. In order for the State and market to properly work, it is necessary to promote a sense of community, first ensured by associations.

Despite the unexpected theoretical premises, therefore, the tendency to universalize values, expectations, and attitudes typical of the growth society is not averted. Anti-utilitarian political strategy is based on three key proposals: reducing working time, unconditional basic income, promoting civil society (Caillé, 1997, 1998, p. 247). These measures will hopefully contribute to restore democracy as a continuous and noninstrumental process. Well, it is not at all obvious that a citizen with income and time spontaneously immolate himself for political and social participation (consumption orgy and holiday dissipation are far more seductive alternatives and, among other things, much more adherent to antiutilitarian intuitions).

The reference to the "measure" (as limit) expressed in the *Revue* number about *alter*-globalization proves to be theoretically weak (Caillé & Insel, 2002). Caillé criticizes the tendency to limitless growth but his goal remains to ensure the maximum power for the greatest number ("la puissance de vivre et d'agir") in the given conditions. The limit would emerge, as already mentioned, by recognizing "reversibility" and "reciprocity." So, the reference to "measure" is only used to ensure the maximum possible dose of power to everyone: power itself is not questioned. Hence, we remain stuck over the cardinal principle of modernity, namely the defense of life itself, regardless of the meaning of life. We still participate in the construction of a neutral arena, in a more sympathetic way, but leaving the system untouched. The anti-utilitarian project is, at the end, the most refined declination of the limitless accessibility regime. Like this one, it doesn't suggest a specific idea of good, but it aims at enabling men (singularly or collectively) to conceive and realize the widest possible number and variety of world visions. This goal is not at all in contradiction with the logic of growth.

Therefore, anti-utilitarianism illusorily fights against a pattern of society (i.e., the modern growth-led regime) that, indeed, has never denied the complexity of the human.

What is implied in the fear of catastrophe?

As we have seen, degrowth's narrative usually starts by evoking the cata-strophe threat. This pivotal argument against the growth society raises several problems, first about the reliability of the scenario. As Wolfgang Sachs argued: "the problem with the catastrophe is that it never occurs."[8] The negative externalities of growth on the environment cause slow and continuous lacera-tions or, at most, limited, punctual disasters. The "great catastrophe" is instead an unlikely hypothesis, but above all useless, since, even if it should occur, no one at that point could learn anything more from it.[9]

The catastrophe stake raises problems first and foremost with respect to the democratic content of the degrowth alternative and the above-mentioned dynamic *legein–teukein*. It assumes that there is a crisis of environmental balance, a crisis of resources, which endangers human existence or, at least, it endangers the perpetuation of the current development pattern. This formu-lation of the challenge produces a technical bias, inconsistent with the idea of people's sovereignty that is at the heart of a real notion of democracy. This bias stems from the fact that, since the ecological crisis cannot be seen with the naked eye, expert knowledge is a prerequisite for its mere "recording." The average citizen, apart from the trouble, more or less disruptive, of general pollution, has no means at his disposal to say that the world is in fact in danger. He can only trust what the experts declare. But after the experts have defined the problem, it is almost inevitable to ask the people who detected it to take the lead for its resolution. It is totally unrealistic to imagine that the experts would limit themselves to saying what the predicament is, or neutrally draw the alternative escape scenarios, hence allowing people to autonomously take a decision. The intrusiveness of technical knowledge (which, of course, is inescapable, to some extent) in the realm of action and regulation is almost innate. But it dispossesses people of their sovereignty and their freedom of opinion concerning their lives. These are determined according to an icy *diktat*, with the chrism of objectivity, issued by science. Only those experts, who are capable of seeing things "from above" can judge the legitimacy of the life models chosen by common people.[10]

Furthermore a basic problem with this view of a pending catastrophe is that if the ecological crisis were to be metabolized in the collective conscious-ness as a shared "reality," the destiny of any sociopolitical course would then be predetermined: any kind of society, of coexistence, of environmental gov-ernance and of organization of our relationship with Planet Earth (regardless of its degree of democratization) would in principle have to seek the same result: "ecological compatibility." This governing fundamental principle is an apolitical axiom, which is supposed to hold priority over any subsequent dis-cussion (more or less democratic) on the idea of a good society. It is a prin-ciple to be upheld under all circumstances; all ideas must obey to that final result. Then, one wonders, if a technocratic or nondemocratic regime is more suitable to deal with an emergency situation, why not choose this instead of a less-effective democratic one? (Nebbia, 2002). An anti-democratic drift is clearly plausible in the pursuit of ecological compatibility.

However, the catastrophe issue can be better understood if treated – to put it ethnomethodologically – as a "research object," rather than as a "resource for research."[11] The pivotal arguments proposed by the degrowth narrative show a general devotion to catastrophe which is now spreading in many areas of our societies, pervading social movements, political perspectives, public arenas, literature, television schedules, entire strands of Hollywood cinematography, etc. It is a fixed idea, a recurring dream, an obsession typical of the inhabitants of advanced capitalist societies. A sort of unconfessable desire that emerges here and there.[12] What leads us to root around for catastrophe?

Our condition of political aphasia is evident: we experience powerlessness in imagining credible political alternatives to the present regime, despite the self-representation, continually reiterated, as inhabitants of the realm of freedom and democracy, in which a degree of individual autonomy has been achieved that was never registered before (Bauman, 1999).

The end of real socialism played a role in the implementation of this state. Its mere presence signaled – regardless of the desirability of that regime – the possibility of an alternative inside the Western civilization field. Despite the extent of the margins of freedom acquired, no lucid person would bet that a radical transformation of the world as we know it today could occur before or after. This is an unheard-of condition compared to only a few decades ago, when it was possible to imagine change, for better or for worse. It is as if we really had reached the best of all possible worlds. We live in what Baudrillard has called the universal equivalence regime, in which every singularity (cultural, social, even individual) is sucked into a homologating code that dissolves any specificity, making it a mere option included in the game of the absolute interchangeability of preferences (Baudrillard, 2001, 2002). This fixity of the present world leaves no way out. It relegates us into a closed horizon, as Bataille, following Freud (1990), had denounced: man needs to escape from himself, from his identity armor; he needs to escape elsewhere. He needs, to be honest, to kill himself.

The more the horizon tightens to every political alternative, imposing the universalist equivalence as a systemic regulatory code, the more the desire for catastrophe spreads, as the only viable way out. The obsession with catastrophe springs from our political aphasia, soliciting us to come back to the ancient, comforting fear of an omnipotent nature, which finally frees us from our unbearable autonomy. A new "escape from freedom" (Fromm, 1994). Taking refuge in the fixed idea of catastrophe is the first symptom of the "political" weakness of degrowth. It means recognizing, in fact, that the strength of the growth-for-growth's-sake regime cannot be contended with an equally attractive alternative, capable of gaining consensus through a physiological struggle in the open field of politics. Therefore, our only option is to claim the alliance with a superior majesty, transcendent and impolitic: "nature," to be precise. We ask nature to carry out the dirty work in our place: to sweep away a life pattern against which we clearly recognize that we do not have enough effective political arguments. Abandoning the growth regime is a "necessity" decreed by nature, not a "choice" made by free men: the mere evocation of the catastrophe as a central argument means abdicating our sovereignty, our autonomy of "qualified" human beings (Arendt, 1951, 1998).

In this sense, degrowth rides the most unhealthy moods on the agenda (which makes it attractive in the short term and weak in the long run), considering them a "reality," rather than the "symptom" of a stronger discomfort to deal with. But the homogeneity of degrowth to the *zeitgeist* is deeper than that. It is rooted in the founding social imaginary of modernity and utilitarianism. Growth – as already mentioned – is first and foremost condemned as a threat to "life," to human survival. Well, the question is: why survive?

The preservation of living beings (from humans to whales) appears to be such an obvious goal that not even a line in degrowth literature is spent to defend its supposed supreme value. The defense of life for life's sake, regardless of and before any question on the sense of life, is launched here as a value in itself, an undisputable moral imperative, that does not need any justification whatsoever. The impending catastrophe does not allow us to indulge in similar questions. But there is a much deeper reason explaining this omission: the subordination of degrowth to the main article of faith of the modern–Western imaginary colonialism (disguised, as usual, as a universal dogma, extra-historical and extra-geographic). That is to say: the sacredness of life itself. This imperative translates the "neutralitarian" root of utilitarian political philosophy:[13] modernity demands an a-teleological political power which would never interfere with the construction of the sense of associated life, since this has to be but the spontaneous result of the interaction among individuals, who alone are given the sovereignty in formulating and fulfilling their own existential project. In such conditions, politics cannot but have a function of mere guarantee for preservation (life for life's sake) or, even better, for cultivation (growth for growth's sake) of the "organic" life of citizens, combined with the administrative regulation of their circulation. We need to limit ourselves to making life grow, so that living beings can be free to do whatever they wish with it. Originally, as we have seen, growth is nothing but the translation of the modern principle of neutrality: it is "rightly" indifferent to whatever aim, except for that of increasing the material possibilities of each one to choose and achieve one's aims. In this sense, the principle of growth for growth's sake is equivalent to the principle of life for life's sake. They are mutually pleonastic. The former can be said to be nothing but a euphoric declination of the latter. For decades we have betted that the best way to defend and sustain life was to head for growth. Today, someone is warning us that this strategy is insufficient when not harmful: therefore, it would be better to head for degrowth.

In short, degrowth remains stuck in the path of "neutralism," life for life's sake, *teukein*'s primacy (Strunz & Bartkowski, 2018). Flapping the threat of catastrophe ("degrowth or collapse," as Bonaiuti asserts (2009; Cochet, 2003; Ariès, 2005), paraphrasing the old motto "socialism or barbarism"), degrowth evokes nothing but the necessity of setting up a world compatible with the life of our species, without saying anything explicit about the sense of such a life, other than in a cursory manner (e.g., arguments such as: "once life becomes less wasteful of energy, it will be more beautiful to live," a hypothesis that is waiting to be substantiated). I argue therefore that degrowth too is a "technique." It is not concerned with the sense of life. It only pays attention to the conditions for life reproduction. In this way, degrowth meets the paradox of democracy. Degrowth does not worry about the restoring of *legein*, but it works like a *teukein*, merely permitting the species and its members to stay alive. Yes, the strategy changes from growth to degrowth, but the goal remains the same: life, beyond all "sense." The neutralitarian regime that we pretend to fight (by candidly denouncing the lack of purposes in growth) is fully reconfirmed. Degrowth does not produce any epistemological difference compared with the utilitarian fundamentals of the growth society. Yet a community can only be "really democratic" if it debates sense and if it allows for a collective creation of an idea of the "good society," concretely implementing it. It is not democratic if all that it does is bend to the goal of preserving its own existence. From this point of view, degrowth makes no difference for democracy compared to growth. It has nothing to say, in itself, about what constitutes a "good society."

Thus, it is not so obvious, as most degrowth thinkers and advocates assume, that degrowth and democracy are co-substantial and go hand in hand towards a shared destiny (Cheynet, 2008; Research & Degrowth, 2010), nor that the two processes can be mutually reinforced by their alliance: a degrowth society will lead to the rebirth of democracy; and a real democratic society will naturally choose degrowth.

As we will see, failure to clarify this conceptual node limits the quality of the criticism of the growth society and it reflects directly and problematically on the design of a degrowth alternative.

The argumentative frame with which the social unsustainability of the growth regime is denounced is also debatable. First, in this case too the technical approach already mentioned prevails. Well-being produced by the growth regime is "unmasked" by data, cold calculations, scientific measurements that denounce its substantial illusoriness. The "discovery" by default of the GDP negative progression recorded in recent years in almost all industrialized countries does not mean that the growth society stops to be largely appreciated and to establish its hegemony: declaring its bankruptcy on the basis of mere budget operations and figures that don't add up is the vice of a critical and disembodied thought, which doesn't meet the feelings of men in flesh and bones, rejecting a social model only on the basis of a technical knowledge.

Second, degrowthers lay the blame on growth for some distortions that it is very difficult to impute to the growth-led regime. This one produces inequalities and injustices, they claim. Well, growth and equality went hand in hand for a long time in welfare societies. If this no longer happens, it is most probably due to the hegemony of neoliberalism and to the coeval misfortune of equality as a social value, after the collapse of the Berlin Wall. It is not necessarily the outcome of the growth myth. It is also doubtful that the weakening of social relations can be attributed to the same cause. Is it a direct and necessary effect of growth or of the sociocultural framework in which it is grafted?

But it is more interesting not to cast doubt on the truth of the assumption rather on its paradoxical feature. That is, the fact that it leaves the model of Western life basically immune, referring however to a concept of life based on the unlimited, infinitely positive quest for "feeling better and better." Modernity has never encouraged having more for having more but having more for being better.

Degrowthers' criticism fits within a more general instance typical of the "reflexive modernity" (Beck et al., 1994). That instance which saves modernity in itself, denouncing some drifts that make contemporary society different from its original project. The ultimate goal remains the quest for immanent well-being: the fact that it can be obtained by increasing the resources produced, decreasing them or, even, stopping to deal with them, is a detail that certainly does not challenge the model of society. The desired scheme, of heading for the highest satisfaction possible – briefly, the anthropological and imaginary structure of modernity – remains completely untouched.

Under these conditions, the strategy of degrowth works only as an artificial breathing device in order to keep a now-exhausted model of society alive.

At the basis of the dominant degrowth vision one still finds the pursuit of well-being by everyone, the increase of the chances to do and be what everyone wants. There is not a common political project, an attempt to restore *legein*, just the amplification of a general enabling *teukein*. Likewise, much of the programmatic and political side of the degrowth movement is nothing more than a list of what we can call "survival techniques," indifferent to the meaning of life (we will return to this in the next chapter).

Therefore, the degrowth proposal remains trapped in the same paradigm of growth and development, although in a reversed form. The goal is always "survival" and/or well-being. If a few years ago this was to be obtained by pushing the accelerator on growth (and thereby increasing the prosperity chances for all), today it should be pursued by choosing degrowth, so that the environment does not crack. Degrowth remains stuck within the paradigm of neutrality, aiming at biological survival, regardless of the sense of life.

I conclude therefore that degrowth, in its current and dominant formulation, does not hold intrinsic properties suitable to resolve the basic crisis of democracy, i.e., the impasse of collective sovereignty over the world, and does not counteract the pervasiveness of *teukein*. On the contrary, degrowth is a new mutation of the hegemony of technique and it leaves the problem of collective sense and democracy unresolved. Degrowth reinforces modernity's view of individual well-being as paramount (generating, in turn, the primacy of life for life's sake) which, paradoxically, is precisely the one that prevents the deployment of collective sovereignty.

The desiring device, aimed at the maximum possible self-satisfaction, in short, the anthropological and imaginary pattern of modernity remains completely untouched. It is basically a mere lexical question. The modern model of man is fully confirmed. In this sense, we do not understand the charge put to degrowthers of yearning for a return to the premodern past. They can only be reproached – as we will see later on – for enveloping the modern anthropological framework in an inconsistent institutional form. But beyond this, degrowth does not aim to subvert the project of modernity: it claims to equip it against new challenges, just like the intellectuals who support a reflexive modernization.

Notes

1 See the links: https://lepassagerclandestin.fr/catalogue/les-precurseurs-de-la-decroissance.html and www.ibs.it/libri/collane/i-precursori-della-decrescita-p200144
2 The two founders made the decision to start up the intellectual venture after having participated the year before in an interdisciplinary debate with philosophers, economists, and psychoanalysts on the topic of "gift exchange." On that occasion they shared the same frustration with other participants. They expressed obstinacy in their profound belief that behind every human action, including gift practices and demonstrations of generosity, we must recognize the strategy of egotistical calculation, and nothing more.
3 In our argumentative process we will make special reference to the declination of the theory of degrowth supplied by Serge Latouche (2007, 2011, 2019). Not simply because of the authoritativeness of the writer, but especially because Latouche's theory – in evoking the idea of a "society of degrowth" (as opposed to the mere "economy of degrowth") – is that which, more than any other, has clearly made room for subtle thinking on the anthropological substratum of the project. Despite the fact that, precisely because of his attention to the anthropological variables, Latouche has been accused by the most demanding modernist theorists (Cheynet, 2008) of winking treacherously at archaic and old-fashioned social repertoires; we will highlight, instead, how his anthropological reference picture does not draw away at all from the foundation imagination of the present time (the same as the one of the society of growth) and that this very circumstance determines the unsustainability of an alternative project. In this sense, if our criticism applies to Latouche, it will apply more so to those, among the supporters of degrowth, who completely exclude the anthropological dimension from their own theoretical horizon, thus postulating an adherence by default to the imaginary bases of the present.
4 Latouche, 2007, p. 14.
5 Latouche, 2007, p. 17.
6 Latouche, 2007, p. 18.
7 "By 'voluntary degrowth' I mean a vision for the future that is promoted because it is regarded as preferable to a growth economy ... a cultural and social critique of society – an alternative 'imaginary' of how society might be" (Davey, 2014).
8 Seminar on degrowth, September 10, 2005, Free School for Social Alternatives, Polvese Island, Trasimeno Lake. Indeed, with this statement Sachs intended to

challenge the ineffectiveness of the catastrophe as a "promotional" tool for degrowth alternative. The catastrophes that daily punctuate television and press reports are instantly metabolized by an omnivorous and indifferent public opinion. Even when they touch us personally, they are removed with diligence and, in any case, we find it hard to recognize them as a direct effect of our lifestyles.

9 Moreover, the weak reliability of the scenario is demonstrated by Latouche when he says, with regard to the so-called ecological footprint, that every human being has a bioproductive space of 1.8 hectares, while today we consume an average of 2.2 hectares per capita (2007, p. 29). One or the other: either Planet Earth is providing us with resources on credit, or the writer – me – is a ghost (and the reader, too). Latouche reveals the improbability of the scenario when he affirms, with regard to the so-called ecological footprint, that each human being has a bioproductive space of 1.8 hectares, while today we consume on average 2.2 hectares per capita (2007, p. 29).

10 We acknowledge that this perspective is completely foreign to Latouche's sensitivity, but in the environmental movement the temptations towards a technical government of the planet, arousing directly from the idea of degrowth, are quite widespread. Let's take, for example, what Giorgio Nebbia (2007) affirms in this regard:

> In the wake of the Georgescu–Roegen writings the invitation to "degrowth" was born, which risks remaining a new fashion if the question is not answered: decrease of who and what? Of the population and the consumption of the "first world" industrialized countries 1,000 million inhabitants, or of the "second world" 2,500 million inhabitants of the rapidly industrializing countries such as China, India and Southeast Asia, or of the 3,000 million inhabitants of the poor and extremely poor "third world"? A decrease in the consumption of the elderly or of young people, of luxury commodities or of survival goods? Using which subjects? In order to answer these questions we need proper statistics of the physical goods available and those that are being lost, and the correct indicators, as an alternative to the deceptive Gross Domestic Product in monetary units, of the relationships between human activities and needs, the distribution of goods and of the physical and natural effect of each human action. Good work to those who will live in the coming decades, we hope for a technological but neotechnical and biotechnical society, with levels of consumption consistent with the natural cycles.

11 On the distinction between research "subject" and research "resource" in ethnomethodology, see Zimmermann and Pollner (1970).

12 "We dreamed of that event ... Yes, 'they' did it, but 'we' desired it" (Baudrillard, 2002, on the Twin Towers attack).

13 As we know, Bentham (1939) argued that the political institution was supposed to deal with the happiness of the great majority, but without ever getting into the concept of happiness chosen by each one. For some people, happiness is making money, for others it might be writing poetry. We often forget this pivotal idea of utilitarianism, blindly reducing the doctrine to a monomaniac inclination to the useful intended in a merely economic sense.

3 Rethinking degrowth through *dépense*

Georges Bataille: the forgotten precursor

For the reasons considered in the previous chapter, the project for degrowth seems to us unsuitable to challenge the complexity of the present regime and to set up an authentic social alternative freed from the growth logic. In our opinion, it is instead necessary to completely reformulate the project for a degrowth society starting from the concept of *dépense* developed in the past century by Georges Bataille in his theory of "the general economy."

Adopting Bataille as the main reference for a reformulation of the degrowth alternative may be a risky move. We are aware of it. Georges Bataille immediately evokes the sulphurous domains of the extreme, eroticism, the fascination for the negative and for evil: far away from the framework of sobriety where degrowth narrative usually lies. Far away, in particular, from the ecological (and social) concern that is the cornerstone of the degrowth alternative. But if the aim is not, as Serge Latouche tirelessly repeats, the deliberate pursuit of a productive recession, rather the implementation of a society freed from the religion of utilitarianism and limitless growth as an end in itself, then Georges Bataille becomes a crucial reference. In spite of the fragmented and asystematic character, his work represents one of the most consistent and radical attempts to unmask the unsustainability of a human consortium founded on the reduction of things and people to their productive ("servile") function, as well as the theoretical domain where the issue of the sacred, that is to say the social practices aimed at taking out social institutions from their utilitarian status, has found the due space:

> My purpose is to show in a series of works and essays ... on the one hand the deep deformations of the general balance that the annual development of industry has brought about, on the other the prospects of an economy not centered on growth.... It will be necessary to introduce new theoretical considerations and to found the general representation of the economic game on the description of the systems in place before the capitalist accumulation. These studies will then have to include a field

generally considered extrinsic to the economy: that of religions, primitive or not, to which the field of the history of the arts is connected.

(Bataille, 1998, p. 279)

Between *décroissance* (degrowth) and *dépense* (expenditure – the Batallian concept we will primarily discuss here) there is an evident assonance in intuitively evoking the attempt to perform a reversion of the "naturally" unilinear path of growth (Stoekl, 2007). Contrasting this regime is the common cause. The unsustainability, inadequacy, and undesirability of the bourgeois growth-led regime are at the core of Bataille's work. For this reason, he is a precious ally of degrowth supporters.

Beyond this staple, however, everything appears upside down. In the Batallian wonderland, many of the beliefs underlying the degrowth thought are literally reversed. If for degrowth advocates the fundamental problem is scarcity (an infinite growth is incompatible with the finite character of the planet's resources), for Bataille the basic problem is abundance (the excess of energy that weighs as a "curse" on living beings, it threatens to destroy them or it simply vanishes in a senseless way). If for degrowth advocates the growth regime is to be condemned for its voracity, which would lead to the depletion of natural resources, for Bataille it must be abandoned because it does not "eat" enough energy. If, finally, for degrowthers it is time to practice the ethics of parsimony and sobriety, for Bataille, on the contrary, it is necessary for men to relearn the art of waste.

> In fact, in my opinion, the use of riches, or more precisely their purpose, is essentially waste: their withdrawal from the production circuit. Now, this truth has not only founded from the beginning the profound human values (those of selflessness) and all the human treasures that the centuries have transmitted to us; but in addition, it is the only truth we could base ourselves on now to solve the problems posed by industrial development. Only the gift without hope of profit, starting by the principle that resources are in excess, can bring the present world out of the impasse.
>
> (1998, p. 279)

Anyway, Georges Bataille is a drug to be taken very carefully. Its benefits can be extraordinary, as are the side effects in terms of sterile aestheticization, which often infects those who let themselves be sucked in by the seductive rhetorical vortices scattered throughout his vast intellectual production. It must be clear that we are dealing with an irregular author and an elusive thinker. He called himself a saint or a madman rather than a philosopher (Bataille, 2002). It is not easy to deal with a madman, but it is almost always worth it. Even more so when the fool is Georges Bataille. His thoughts never add up. Ambiguity is the key. Shedding light on his vision and showing its fruitfulness for a degrowth alternative is, nevertheless, our task.

Georges Bataille (1897–1962) built his intellectual path outside the academy and beyond all disciplinary boundaries. Writer, novelist, essayist, philosopher, anthropologist, sociologist, economist, etc.: the expressive codes he used to explore the obsessions generated by a life in constant contact with death and illness are innumerable.

His childhood was spent in Billom (where he was born on September 10, 1897) and then in Reims with a blind, syphilitic, almost paralyzed father who made him a lazy and insolent child. He evaded the depressive context of his family by devoting himself to studies and to Catholic religion. He escapes the horror of the Great War, first by disappearing from Reims bombed by the Germans (where, however, his father remained mortally trapped), then, thanks to a hint of tuberculosis, avoided conscription. He entered the Catholic seminary in 1917, but the priestly vocation soon faltered. He then continued his studies in Madrid, where he witnessed the death of the bullfighter Manuel Granero (in a bullfight; the memory of this disturbing event was to remain with him). Returning to France in 1922, he was hired as a clerk in the National Library of Paris. These were intense years, marked by the attendance of the surrealist movement, by psychoanalysis, and by the equivocal ravines of the city, which inspired his first obscene novels. In 1928 he married the actress Sylvia Maklès, with whom he had a daughter, before embarking on a very tormented relationship with Colette Peignot, whose death in 1938 devastated Bataille. He became chief editor of the magazine *Documents*, which welcomed defectors of the surrealist movement, making André Breton go on a rampage. But with the latter (and with Roger Caillois) he later founded *Contre-attaque*, a more "political" magazine, which targeted the anti-revolutionary tendencies of the socialist and communist movements of the time.

Bataille's most significant experience as social sciences scholar was founding the Collège de Sociologie, between 1937 and 1939, jointly with Roger Caillois, Michel Leiris, Pierre Klossowski, and others. The declared intent was to highlight the critical potential of social sciences in their application to modern society, assuming the "sacred" as the founding dimension of social existence. In this sense, the group did not stand as a simple scientific community, but more properly as a "moral community," welded through periodic public discussions. In parallel, the "esoteric" experience of the *Acéphale* review developed: here the critique of the modern fetish of the free, conscious, and rational individual reached its most virulent expression.

From the second postwar period until 1962, the year of his death, Bataille led a modest life, as an occasional librarian, due to his perennial state of illness, while continuing to write and publish sumptuous and unclassifiable works.

L'économie générale

As already mentioned, Bataille's work holds, in our opinion, a fundamental coherence even if it appears fragmented and unsystematic. If it is an exaggeration to say, as often happens with authors, that he always wrote the same book, it is nevertheless legitimate to hypothesize that his thought, beyond the specific objects of reflection, the different styles, and the several genres frequented, rotated almost obsessively around the same center of attraction (Rella, 2003). That is: the disintegration of the "totality" (from the continuum nature–culture to community), from which the modern hubris of the utilitarian growth springs, reducing the world. Knowing this – and also in consideration of the limits of this work (completely incongruous with respect to the vastness of the Bataillian work) – we will focus on a specific side of Georges Bataille's work: what he called "the general economy," with an unusual scientific and systematic claim (obviously never fulfilled). The works that fit in this effort begin with *La notion de dépense*, the essay appeared for the first time in *La critique sociale* in January 1933 (no. 7).

There are at least seven different versions of this first essay. Starting from the notion of *dépense*, the theoretical project of the general economy will find its first fragmentary versions in the essays "L'Économie à la mesure de l'univers" ("The economy tailored to the universe") (Bataille, 1976a) and "La limite de l'utile" ("The limits of the useful") (1976b) and will materialize in a more organic form in the work *La part maudite* ("The accursed share") (1988). This was followed by a second part entitled *Histoire de l'érotisme* ("The history of eroticism") (1976c) and the third and final part entitled *La Souveraineté* ("On Sovereignty") (1976d).

Dépense relates to the concepts of "transience" – *Vergänglichkeit* (on which Benjamin and Adorno dwelled) – and above all of Freud's "death drive" (Baudrillard, 1976). He draws more explicitly from the *Essai sur le don* ("The Gift") by Marcel Mauss (Bataille attended his lessons), in particular his reflections about the *potlach*.

In *La notion de dépense*, Bataille focuses on consumption activity, characterized by two distinct functions and modes. The first is necessary for the conservation and the reproduction of life. The second is used for nonproductive expenditures: "luxury, mourning, wars, religion, the construction of sumptuous monuments, games, spectacles, the arts, perverse sexual activity (i.e., deviated from generative ends)" (Bataille, 2003, p. 44). This second side corresponds, from the point of view of the human being, to *dépense* (dissipation, expenditure in pure loss, without return or gain): "[I]t is necessary to use the term *dépense* only for these unproductive forms, excluding all the consumer modalities which are in fact intermediate steps for the goal of production" (p. 44). It designates the nonservile activities, i.e., not aimed at the conservation, the reproduction and the growth of the living being, but which are ends in themselves, which coincide, more specifically, with a loss (they are generated by the loss). The larger the expenditure, the foremost its meaning.

This second part of consumption activity is, for Bataille, fundamental. It includes decisive functions and meanings, which will be explored later, especially in "The Accursed Share," where the *dépense* issue is approached on a general level, extended to biological processes.

As we have already anticipated, Bataille starts from a matter of fact: the abundance of energy that invests the planet and its inhabitants. This abundance is essentially ensured by the sunlight radiation on earth. Energy released by the sun profusely pours on living beings. Plants, animals, men are able to catch only an infinitesimal part of the circulating energy for the satisfaction of their vital needs, that is for biological reproduction.[1] But these needs are not sufficient to capture all the available energy, therefore living beings catch and spend an additional share of energy to "grow," thus going beyond the threshold of the accomplishment of mere survival processes. But their growing capacity is also limited. The living system is not able to dispose of all the available energy. Thus, the surplus energy, which cannot be used by living beings due to their physiological limits, builds up. It starts circulating and pressing on earth. Finding no utilization, the surplus undertakes a process of gradual dissipation, until it burns out. If we consider only the "biological" domain, we can define *dépense* as the dissipation of the share of energy that exceeds the absorption capacity of living beings. As Bataille puts it:

> The living organism ... receives in theory more energy than it is necessary to sustain life: the surplus energy (wealth) can be employed for the growth of a system (such as an organism); if the system cannot anymore grow or if the surplus cannot be entirely absorbed by its growth, then we assist at a loss without return; surplus is spent, willingly or not, gloriously or in a catastrophic way.
>
> (2003, p. 73)

The process, simple and almost mechanical, has important implications when we move from the biological sphere to the anthropological domain: from this point of observation, the energy could be redefined as the fuel of the action; more specifically, the fuel that "calls us to act," the mere presence of which urges men to choose for it (and, if necessary, to justify) a destination.

Like all other living beings, man is able to spend for his sustenance and growth only a tiny portion of the available energy. At this stage, the use of energy takes a distinctly "servile" character. Man is driven by a natural impulse, by his needs, like every other living organism. Intentionality is not needed. There is no need to activate those distinctive dimensions of the human being that consist of reflection, of the elaboration of a sense, and of political mediation. Man is on this side of consciousness. He is a thing (although animated) among things.

Acting *dépense*

Problems arise when we stand before the residual energy that exceeds the amount needed for servile use. The most conspicuous share. In fact, surplus energy claims a "sovereign" use, emancipated from the instrumental relation with life reproduction (Hegel, 1976). The meeting with excess energy is a crucial time, as it tests the very consistency of the human, after the satisfaction of those natural needs that assimilate man with all other living organisms, animals, and plants. This moment marks the transition from unconsciousness to consciousness, from the animal to the human. Here, the state of urgency that in the human being suspends all questions on the ultimate meaning of life, the world, and of the general biological system in which he instinctively and unthinkingly works for the procurement of vital resources, finally ends.

The surplus immediately appears as an "accursed share." Why? There are a lot of reasons.

First of all, its pressure on the world is in itself an inexhaustible source of anxiety: it places humankind before the question of freedom, of choice. There are no more "natural" indications on how to use energy. Instinct does not decide for us anymore. Humankind must now elaborate a sense, an end, in the name of which to draw the fuel of action and channel it into canons of value autonomously designed. It is necessary to decide the destination for the fuel, on the basis of a philosophical intention, of a project, which can no longer be drawn from the mere automatism of natural processes. By using surplus energy, we qualify ourselves as human beings. Humankind is called to mark the world with its own imprint: tell me how you use the surplus and I'll tell you who you are.

> In the sphere of human activity the dilemma takes this form: either most of the available resources (i.e., work) are used to fabricate new means of production – and we have the capitalist economy (accumulation, the growth of wealth) – or the surplus is wasted without trying to increase production potential – and we have the festive economy. In the first case, human value is a function of productivity; in the second, it is linked to the most beautiful outcomes of art, poetry, i.e.,: the full growth of human life. In the first case, we only care about the time to come, subordinating the present time to future; in the second, only the present instant becomes relevant, and life, at least from time to time and as much as possible, is freed from the servile considerations that dominate a world devoted to the growth of production.
>
> (Bataille, 1998, p. 277)

It is the different ways of using the surplus that determines, in fact, the specific characters and differences of human consortia in time and space. The surplus can be spent in sacrifices or in glory, in religious asceticism or in the festive *re-ligare*, in war or in peace (as, for example, the teachings of Tibetan society, assigning it almost entirely to the maintenance of an important monastic caste).

If we fail in the use of excess energy, then this means that we are unable to create the meaning of our life, to have a philosophical intentionality. The issue of freedom is strictly linked to the question of nothingness: it reveals the absence of "natural" indications on the road to take and on the destination of man's path in the world. The surplus energy "calls" him to act, in a context in which "nothingness" is the only certainty.

The fact that surplus goes to die – and here we meet a further factor of curse – reveals the "infinite emptiness of all" (to quote the Italian poet Leopardi). The general economy warns us that the destiny of energy (the fuel of action) is dissipation. Everything turns into nothing. Therefore, even the servile activity, revised now by "conscious" individuals, appears as a senseless rush. The sphere of utility becomes unlivable, when reconsidered by an aware actor. It appears as a service activity to a biological machine whose movement has no destination. In the servile domain one can dwell only on condition of being unconscious.

Since the excess energy weighs like a permanent threat of dissolution on every human construction, civilizations engage in a continuous struggle against "nature" (the cradle of dissipation). They tend to raise solid boundaries towards it, to disseminate a whole series of prohibitions and prescriptions that keep negative energy (excrement, nonprocreative sexuality, death, everything that has not a functional–productive use) at a safe distance. Sewers are buried, cemeteries are located on the edge of the city, sexual activity is hidden in the secret rooms. All this "natural" matter causes repugnance and horror, precisely because it symbolically embodies the threat of dissolution, the energy that overwhelms every "product" of man. When he is not concerned with circumscribing, arranging, or deliberately destroying the surplus energy, this one can turn on him in a catastrophic way.

> The disclaimer changes nothing in the final outcome. We can ignore it, forget it: in any case, the soil on which we live is nothing but a field of multiple destructions. Our ignorance has only this incontestable effect: it leads us to *undergo* what, if we knew, we could *act* in our own way. It deprives us of the choice of an exudation that we might like. Above all it allows men and their works to fall prey to catastrophic destruction. Since, if we do not have the strength to destroy the surplus energy ourselves, it cannot be used; and like an intact animal that cannot be trained, it destroys us, and we pay the costs of the inevitable explosion.
>
> (Bataille, 2003, p. 75)

Nevertheless, the surplus has a double face. Ambiguity is its basic feature. It provides pain and delight. It is an accursed and, at the same time, a blessed share, where Eros gets the best of Thanatos. The accursed share, more precisely, has a strong power of attraction for man. It is not just a disgrace to keep away, but also (above all, we would say) a glorious chance. First, as we have already noted, the surplus challenges us to get out of our condition of servitude and submission (to our natural "needs" and to profit, to productive activity, where we sacrifice enjoyment in the name of a future result). The "call for acting," generated by the mere presence of excess fuel, forces us to become autonomous, to self-qualify as human beings, to distance ourselves and to differentiate ourselves from the biological machine that employs us as mere living beings. Man builds his own destiny. From another point of view, the surplus of energy provides us with the chance of finally enjoying the world, of being "sovereign."

> Sovereignty is characterized by the consumption of wealth, as opposed to work, to servitude, which produce wealth without consuming it. The sovereign consumes and does not work, while, at the antipodes of sovereignty, the slave, the man without assets work and reduce their consumption to the strict minimum, to products without which they could neither survive nor work.
>
> (Bataille, 2009, pp. 13–14)

Second, the encounter with the surplus allows man to join the "totality." What does it mean? Man is separated twice: in the servile, while behaving like an animal, a "natural" entity, he is totally focused on himself, since survival is his only concern. He is therefore detached from the totality he belongs to. Awareness (once escaped from the darkness of the need regime) makes this condition unlivable, since man discovers himself alone in the middle of nowhere; he realizes that he is a fragment alienated from his whole. Hence, at this stage, a sort of separation emerges between *micro* and *macro*, singularity and totality, but always within the sphere of nature. Another separation then raises between nature and culture, which is necessary to manage the surplus once the servile threshold has been crossed. To be a man, as we have underlined, he has to remove nature and, in particular, the surplus destructive power. This separation is by definition "unnatural." The surplus removal, in order to avoid self-destruction, is obtained at the price of a disjunction from the totality, which leaves man alone in the silence of the universe. In both situations, the surplus is a source of attraction as it alludes to the possibility that, by welcoming it, we can reconnect to the "whole," we can return to mother nature's belly, where the hope of rediscovering the sense that binds everything lies, where the separated fragments finally merge.

In short, energy surplus repels and attracts us. It imposes with its destructive threat a separation from nature and, at the same time, it allows us to regain naturality. It is at the same time what threatens to destroy man and what promises to give him meaning, to give him access to the mystery of the universe, to the comfort of totality, where the original laceration (the cutting of the umbilical cord), finally, is sutured. Whichever way you look at it, you can't escape the accursed share. It is the crest between the destruction and the realization of man. Thanks to surplus energy, we acquire the awareness of nothingness and, at the same time, the chance to escape from it. It allows the maximum explosion of nonsubordinate life and simultaneously it channels our tension towards death: to be *and* not to be. It is the ridge above which man declares: "I freely am" and "I free myself from the pain of being." He becomes reconciled with the quiet of natural matter, regaining the totality from which he originates and opposing his state of singularity in the emptiness, of senselessness and split outgrowth.

For this reason, *dépense* takes a leap: from nature to society. "Acting *dépense*" means avoiding annihilation by the surplus energy and then trying, welcoming it, to recover what Bataille calls the "intimacy" with nature, with the totality, in order to experience the "miracle," to sovereignly enjoy the world, beyond the profit slavery.

With *dépense* man is a double agent. On the one hand he attempts to "contain" the excess energy (a constitutive move for every civilization: the expulsion of the negative, of excrement, of nonexploitable residue of every productive activity, and of every activity or entity not "useful" for the reproduction of life), on the other hand he sets up practices and rituals for *dépense*, in order to deliberately dissipate the excess energy. All human societies (or, at least, as we shall see, all premodern societies) have been concerned with setting up *dépense* paths, to defuse extra-servile energy. These patterns – always based on the ambivalent game of attraction and repulsion towards nature – have multiple degrees of sophistication and they have several uses. We can summarize the functions covered until now.

Symbolic use: dépense aims, first and foremost, at "humanizing" the surplus dissipation, subtracting it from the uncontrolled domination of natural processes and returning it to culture and symbolism. In this way, dissipation is tamed and framed in an autonomously elaborated meaning.

> In their most eminent form, literature and theater ... provoke anguish and horror by the symbolic representations of a tragic loss (decay or death); in their minor form, they provoke laughter by representations whose structure is similar, but which exclude certain elements of seduction.
>
> (Bataille, 2003, p. 46)

Going towards death, natural energy is marked by a principle of dissipation that generates in human beings a wound very difficult to suture. It produces an inexplicable catastrophe. The fact must therefore be taken over and collectively elaborated. *Dépense* rituals have the function of symbolically welcoming the catastrophe included in the natural *dépense*, without having a "real" annihilation.

See for example what happens in competitive games:

> In the various competitive games, the loss, in general, occurs under complex conditions. Considerable sums of money are spent on the maintenance of premises, animals, equipment or men. Thus, a big amount of energy is spent as much as possible in order to cause a sense of wonder, in any case with an infinitely greater intensity than in productive enterprises. The danger of death is not avoided and, on the contrary, it constitutes the object of a strong unconscious attraction.
>
> (Bataille, 2003, p. 45)

It is the same mechanism interpreted by Freud (1990) as a symptom of the "death drive": the fact that the child voluntarily loses the object of his game (the spool) and he then suffers its disappearance is a simulated way (i.e., by himself "controlled" and acted in a fictitious framework) of reviving the unsustainable trauma of the mother's abandonment. The ritual of *potlach*, widespread among the Native American tribes along the Northwest coasts and analyzed by Marcel Mauss (1950) in his essay on the gift, foresaw the deliberate destruction – in a competitive frame – of precious goods, often corresponding to a value of half the annual crop. The "natural" catastrophe thus becomes meaningful: acting it out directly, men re-signify dissipation to attest their prestige against rival groups. The more you waste, the more you earn in social glory. The surplus destructive potential is employed to strengthen social ties.

Sacrificial function: dépense practices allow man to escape the utilitarian, bio-logical–functional dimension, to access the sacred. In the servile realm, life is deprived of meaning; it is hetero-directed by needs, therefore folded in the unintentional self-reproduction. For a conscious man, the realm of the useful is in itself unlivable. For this reason, man spasmodically tries to escape from the earthly dimension in search of that place where – he bets – things come together in a unity of meaning. The place kept in the safe of the sacred.[2] *Dépense* is the practice that allows this translation and here arises in the form of "sacrifice": the destruction of an object or the killing of a living being aims at erasing their servile status. They are destroyed as "useful things" or "useful beings" and they are carried out in the dimension of the sacred, symbolically re-connected to the whole they belong to. This is the most proper meaning of sacrifice: "in the etymological sense of the term, [it] is nothing more than the production of sacred things" (Bataille, 2003, p. 43), by their ritual destruction.

> From the beginning, it appears that sacred things are constituted by a loss: in particular, the success of Christianity must be explained by the value assigned to the theme of the infamous crucifixion of the child of God who brings human anguish to a representation of the loss and of the decay without limits.
>
> (Bataille, 2003, p. 43)

Also, poetry has to be considered as a form of sacrifice:

> The term "poetry," which applies to the less degraded, less intellectual-ized forms of expression of a state of loss, can be considered as a synonym of *dépense*: it means, in fact, in the most precise sense, creation by means of loss. Its meaning is therefore close to that of sacrifice.
>
> (Bataille, 2003, p. 46)

Connective function: the sacrificial function is more openly revealed in what we can define as the *dépense* connective function (with nature). If in the symbolic function we see an attempt to tame expenditure, by its simulated re-enactment, here it is almost the opposite, i.e., the attempt to plunge into the surplus vortex, which leads directly to the life mystery, namely to the recovery of the "intimacy" relationship with nature, to be at one with it and no longer separate entities, thrown into meaninglessness. Here *dépense* works as a bridge to the heart of nature, allowing man to merge in his womb. Eroticism and religion (two dimensions placed at the antipodes in public discourse) have in common this same function. For Bataille, eroticism is "the approval of life right into death" (Bataille, 1991), that is, surrendering to the fate of the surplus. Religion, with its apparatus of rituals, prohibitions, monuments, works consecrated to deity, makes excess energy the communication channel with the mystery of nature.

Sovereign function: in its most eminent meaning, *dépense* is "sovereign life":

> The sovereign really enjoys the products of this world beyond his needs: here lies his sovereignty. We say that the sovereign (or the sovereign life) begins when, once the necessary is assured, the possibilities of life are opened without limits. Conversely, the enjoyment of possibilities not justified by utility is sovereign (utility: that which has as its aim the productive activity). Beyond utility is the realm of sovereignty. In other words, we can say that it is servile to use the present time for the benefit of the future.
>
> (Bataille, 2009, p. 14)

Enjoying the world, beyond any concern for the future and for its own survival, is constitutively an evanescent experience, which follows the dissipative destiny of energy. The feeling of freely enjoying the world is therefore a sort of "miracle" that for a moment takes us away from terrestrial subordination and puts us in connection with the other, the heterogeneous, the totality of the universe.

> We must satisfy our needs, we suffer if we cannot do it, but as long as it is necessary, we do nothing but follow the animal injunction in ourselves. Beyond need, the object of desire is, humanly, the *miracle*, it is the sovereign life, beyond the necessity characterized by suffering. This *miraculous element, which fascinates us*, can simply be sun shining which transfigures a miserable road on a spring morning. (Which also the poorest, though hardened by necessity, sometimes prove.) It may be the wine, from the first glass to the intoxication that submerges us. More generally, this miracle, to which all of humanity aspires, manifests itself in the form of beauty, of wealth; but also in that of violence, of funeral or sacred sadness; finally, in the form of glory.
>
> (Bataille, 2009, 15)

Pure (or destructive) function: prior to the symbolic forms above mentioned, artistic productions involve a real loss:

[they] must be divided into two broad categories, the first of which consists of architectural constructions, music, and dance. This category involves a *real* expenditure.

(Bataille, 2003, p. 46)

The *dépense* pure cut consists, in fact, in really and physically eliminating from the scene the distressing presence of surplus energy, therefore the call to being and acting. It allows, after all, removing the view of nothingness. The symbolic game is here abolished, together with the attempt to join the totality. Here we have the pure and simple destruction of the surplus, i.e., the refusal to act in the absence of meaning. Indeed, symbolic function and pure function are inextricably co-involved. It is not possible to separate them. The *potlach* is at the same time the symbolic domestication of the surplus energy and the destruction of resources that call men to act beyond the servile realm. It is the same duplicity that we find in the Freudian death drive. The child loses the bobbin both to tame the pain, and to give himself, literally, the death, to disappear from the scene and, therefore, to finally meet the stillness of the matter, regaining a state of unconsciousness that liberates him from the sight of nothingness (Recalcati, 2010). The instantaneous death pain frees us from the persistent pain of meaningless life, which ends in its mere self-reproduction. Just as *décroissance* has an assonance with *décroyance* (stop believing), in the same way *dépense* recalls "de-thinking," a thought divestment on which the Italian comedian Carmelo Bene has built his theatrical poetry (Bene, 1995).

These different functions of the *dépense* emerge here and there in the works of Bataille. However, we must keep in mind that the hand-to-hand with energy never ends. The surplus is reproduced continuously. It is not eliminable once and for all and it is not just what remains from the servile activity. As we have seen, the employment of excess energy qualifies human societies, gives them a specific identity (they become warrior societies, oriented towards mysticism, etc.). But choosing a specific path, a destination of the surplus, necessarily means setting boundaries, creating an external land, generating an "other,"[3] excluding possibilities, etc. All this material becomes new surplus that starts to press on society. This means that while on the one hand inaction allows the surplus to proliferate, on the other, even the determination towards a particular employment of the surplus creates by itself a new surplus. The issue cannot be resolved once and for all. The accursed share is a constant presence in human life. The "decision" about the use of the surplus establishes a separation from the "totality." What remains outside necessarily becomes an "accursed share" we have to deal with. In other words, it generates a renewed "nostalgia for the totality" that returns to burden human existence.

Growth in the light of the general economy

In the light of the general economy it is possible to clearly identify the under-lying problem of the "growth society" born with modernity and on this basis to propose a reformulation of the degrowth project, amending some incon-sistencies of its dominant form today.

The growth society stands on the removal of the problem of energy and its surplus. Indeed, it is based on the exaltation of the servile moment. In this sense, Malthus's concerns for the presumed geometric progression of the population compared with the merely arithmetic progression of resources are paradigmatic. As we saw in the first chapter, much of the historical recon-structions about the origins of modernity (especially the materialistic ones) highlight a situation of urgency for life, for the survival of the species, arising from a sudden demographic explosion (hence, of social needs), while the pro-duction capacity remains the same. This imbalance has produced the decon-struction of traditional community frameworks, of what Illich called the "vernacular" realm, whose symbolic codes did not allow to face the new challenge for survival (Illich, 1973; Samerski, 2018). Individuals had therefore to detach from the tribal and communitarian glue in order to autonomously undertake new action paths aimed at better valuing the natural resources and thus satisfying their needs, no longer fulfilled by the existing collective bodies. This approach to earthly resources is unheard of in the history of humanity:

> In no case does fortune have the function of *freeing the owner from need*. It functionally remains (together with his owner) *at the mercy of a need for unbounded loss* that is endemic in a social group.
>
> (Bataille, 2003, p. 50)

The birth of the growth society is therefore marked by the implosion of the communitarian totality. The individual begins to wander in search of the means of survival. This becomes its dominant occupation. It loses contact with the totality. The impossibility of the community in the modern era con-stitutes, as mentioned above, the fundamental issue that frames the entire work of Bataille.

Community diffraction is assimilated by Bataille to the sun's extinction. The warmth and the dazzling light of the sun, Bataille remarks, envelops all the objects it illuminates, gathering them under the same color. The illumi-nated object is no longer in itself, it becomes invisible, it disappears into the light received, becoming a mere exponent of a beauty *octroyé* from the solar beacon, at the same time homologating with the other objects exposed to the same light. At the center of the scene shines the illuminating splendor, not the illuminated object, which disappears in its blunder. In the growth society, this is intolerable. The object (the individual, in this case) must be subtracted from solar heteronomy to be returned to its own light: the illumination pro-duced by itself on itself. Having no longer the community comfort (which provided for his livelihood), then the individual entirely falls back to the urgency for survival.

We have seen, in this sense, David Riesman's (1950) narrative on the passage from the tradition-directed man, which does nothing but reiterate the customs inherited from his group, to the inner-directed man, who personally elaborates ambitious goals which he pursues with determination throughout the course of his life. Marshall Sahlins (1974), overturning the accepted ideas, also shows that "rich" modern societies are in fact characterized by a mentality of scarcity and, vice versa, "underdeveloped" archaic communities were almost universally impregnated by an "abundance mentality." In short, modernity is marked by the amplification of the servile moment and gets rid of the sovereign dimension, removing from its horizon the surplus energy issue. Everything is reabsorbed by the survival enterprise. All of this reinforces a wrong perception of the state of energy in the living system and anyway it doesn't affect the mechanics of dissipation at all:

> The centrality of necessity arises for the particular living being, or for the limited groups of living beings. But man is not only the separated being who disputes his share of resources to the living world or to other men.... If he denies it, as he continually is obliged to do by the conscience of a necessity, of the indigence characterizing the separated being (who incessantly lacks resources, who is only an eternal needy), his denial doesn't change anything in the dynamic of global energy: this builds up without limits in the productive forces; in the end like a river in the sea, it must escape us and get lost for us.
>
> (Bataille, 2003, p. 75)

The development of the individualization process reduces the collective ability to manage energy and, in particular, to work off the surplus by ritual forms of *dépense* (the collective body becomes a sort of functional, soulless hub, as is well described in the classical works by Elias, Durkheim, Simmel). Surplus management is no longer a collective issue; the individual is now the exclusive holder of each sovereign act. He autonomously takes his determinations about the use of the over-servile portion of the circulating energy.

If this is the institutional response, on a more properly philosophical or, better, ideological level, modern narrative prescribes that the accursed share, although individually managed, must be spent in moral, intellectual, and civil growth. No more *dépense*, no vulgar waste, but an active search for a moral sense to be attached to one's earthly path. The modern subject, already charged with the unbearable weight of the surplus, is then invited to use extra-servile time for his moral perfection.

Needless to say, this is a completely inadequate reply to the issue, given its relevance. Both on the political–institutional side (the burden uploaded on the individual) and on the ideological–moral level (the surplus must be employed for the search for meaning), modernity does not provide credible ways out of the anguish generated by the surplus. This *"manque,"* this lack of response generates multiple consequences in Western societies, of tactical adjustments or, if one prefers, a series of "real answers," against the merely ideological ones made available. We highlight, in particular, three answers: one concerning the shared imaginary, another on the institutional side, the last one aimed at the functional relocation of the "removed" surplus. All these answers are interpretable, following Durkheim (1960), as forms of solidification of the effervescences occurred in the *statu nascenti* of modernity.

The first answer coincides with the exasperation of the original servile moment, that is to say the tension towards unlimited economic "growth."

> Our civilization was formed under the primacy of accumulation, of the consecration of wealth to the increase of production potential. Our moral and political conceptions are still dominated by a principle: the excellence of the development of productive forces.
>
> (Bataille, 1998, p. 278)

The emphasis placed on servilism, in fact, is a strategy for removing the impending surplus. Making the original emergency situation eternal, giving absolute primacy to the activities necessary for survival (and for growth, that represents, as already hypothesized, its euphoric declination) and transforming them in a real collective obsession, allows us to forget the issue of the sense of action.

> At first this prolific movement halted the war activity by absorbing the essential of the surplus: the development of modern industry determined the relative period of peace from 1815 to 1914. The development of productive forces, the growth of resources, made it possible at the same time the rapid demographic multiplication of advanced countries (it is the carnal aspect of the bony structure represented by the proliferation of factories). But in the long run the growth that technical innovations made possible became difficult. In its turn it became the generator of an increased surplus.
>
> (Bataille, 2003, p. 76)

The perpetuation of the survival engagement frees us from that state of paralysis that raises before the call to "be" pronounced by the impending surplus. Staying an animal, man is liberated from the fatigue of the human.

Here returns the "ideological genesis of need" as Baudrillard (1972) called it, that is the erasing of any symbolic function of the object and its reduction to a mere commodity. A process that goes hand in hand with the reduction of the individual to his supposed innate needs. Since individual desires, motivations, and sense are no longer actualizations of the coercion exercised by the community, the actor recognizes his pure essence, beyond the social ties, in his own needs: they are a new source of determination, rationally identifiable, not vitiated by symbolic rubbish. At the molecular level, the mechanism produces a long-term toxic dependence from commodities. At the molar level, instead, we see the transformation of the potential energy surplus into an alleged situation of "real" scarcity of the available resources and of danger for the environmental balances.

Second, as we have seen in the previous chapters, institutions adopt more and more the regulatory principle of life for life's sake. The modern "democratic" institutions, against their legitimating theory, are no longer an arena for collective discussion on the "meaning" of life, on the sense of being together, on what is "good," and on how to achieve it, but they become a mere neutral machine, passive before each person's determinations, only aimed at ensuring exclusively the protection, the reproduction, the promotion and the valorization of the species biological life. Life itself expels the collective construction of its meaning from the public arena. As already underlined, it will then be the individuals, with their free will, to decide on how to use the surplus and therefore which sense to add to their existential path. This is the meaning of the "biopolitical" turn considered, albeit from a different and very questionable perspective, by Foucault (1976, pp. 119–142).

The third answer concerns the *dépense* destiny. It becomes more and more a real self-dissipation practice. In spite of the pretense to spend surplus energy for civil and moral growth, *dépense* is not at all buried in the darkness of tradition. It is simply kicked off the "official" public arena, "privatized" and hidden. Individuals take charge of the expenditure function (once acted out by collectivity in the eminent moments of its rituals), by coasting trade practices: from perverse sexuality to alcoholism, from gambling to conspicuous consumption, etc. Bataille called them the "shameful belching" of the petty bourgeoisie. In the bourgeois era there is no longer the eminent and sumptuous collective *dépense*, but the private dissolution informally consumed in the secret rooms, under the hood of shame, far from public visibility.

> Man's glorious expenditure was brought back to the extent of commercial exploitation.... The form of individual expenditure, which excludes the true splendor, is the only admitted by capitalist production. It is oriented by the mass-produced objects; the simulacrum replaces luxury.... In fact, the individual without social ties cannot aspire to splendor. If he succumbs to the fascination of luxury, he does so without tact: he destroys the sense of splendor. Comfort and boredom are the result of this ever-greater poverty of wealth.
>
> (Bataille, 2000, p. 82)

Bataille has not had time to see that these forms of *dépense*, especially since the second postwar period, with the advent of electronic media, mass culture, and consumer society, have actually ceased to be experienced in the secret rooms and now permanently connote the Western regime out in the open: this is what elsewhere we have called "demodernization" (Romano, 2008), evoked by a long series of authors (from Baudrillard to Bell, from Maffesoli to Magatti) and consisting of a sort of labor division between the economic system – which continues to function according to the usual competitive mechanisms of the capitalist market – and the cultural system, which instead derails towards an ethic of immediate enjoyment, unbridled consumption and values reversibility. Private *dépense* no longer needs to hide and, as we will see later, it is increasingly becoming a pillar of "techno-nihilist" capitalism (Magatti, 2009, 2012).

Despite this form of acknowledgment, *dépense* practices continue to be staged within a degraded frame, by no means appropriate to the importance of surplus employment. The anxiety generated by the burden of surplus energy doesn't find, in this context, a suitable chance of disposal but only palliative responses, thus it inexorably spreads.

> [W]e use surplus to multiply "services" that facilitate life, and we are led to reabsorb some of it in the increase of hours of free time. But these diversions have always been insufficient: their existence in *excess* has always voted multitudes of human beings and large amounts of useful goods to the destruction of wars.
>
> (Bataille, 2003, 75)

Degrowth in the light of *dépense*

It is clear that Bataille's reasons against the growth society are very different from those circulating in degrowth literature and part of degrowthers' political perspective. According to Bataille, the basic point for us is the removal, in our civilization, of the surplus issue:

> Men ensure subsistence or avoid suffering not because these functions by themselves bring about a sufficient result, but in order to access the insubordinate function of free *dépense*.
>
> (2003, p. 59)

Constitutively, growth society is condemned to remain nailed in the servile dimension, even when the objective conditions (abundance and productive saturation) do not justify its primacy.

As we shall see in detail in the next chapter, the servile foundation is so leathery that growth society is able to get rid of its own institutional forms when they threaten to definitely liberate citizens from the need's yoke: in fact, the vertical welfare regime collapses when it makes the individual productive effort vain, disentangling Western citizens from the servile realm.

The nonresponse to the surplus issue has a lot of implications: it means to remain in the animality, but paradoxically without "intimacy" with nature (that is, occupied with the challenge of one's own singular survival and separated from the totality which one belongs to); anxiety grows, due to the

burden of surplus energy on a living being incapable of responding to the call
to being and acting; it means exposing man to the risk that the surplus energy
not disposed of turns against him in the form of a real catastrophe; it means to
remain separated from nature, as well as from the community as a whole; it
means to renounce enjoying the world, after having satisfied the basic needs,
that is, renouncing to a sovereign and glorious life; it means suffering nothingness without acting on it; it means not accepting death. And much more.
A society developing beyond "growth" is therefore necessary. The project for
a degrowth society could largely benefit from the metabolization of the
Bataillian perspective. Degrowth and *dépense* should go hand in hand: a real
degrowth society has to incorporate the functions played by *dépense*.

Dépense is therefore a key concept for thinking a way out of the growth
society. Paradoxically, however, it does not appear among the epistemological pillars of mainstream theoretical reflection on degrowth, nor is it a source
of inspiration for counter-growth movements. The only relevant exception is
represented by the editors of the degrowth vocabulary that in their postface
("From austerity to dépense") suggest adopting *dépense* as a pivotal tool for
degrowth theory and practice, challenging the perplexities and the discontent
of a wide share of the movement (D'Alisa et al., 2014). Obviously, their
generous attempt has not been followed and probably not even understood,
because an authentic metabolization of *dépense* would imply the deconstruc-
tion of the cognitive frame at the basis of the degrowth thought. It is not possible to implement a simple collation of Bataille's thought to the degrowth
perspective. Truly embracing Bataille's narrative would entail the dismantling
of the cognitive frame supporting the criticism of the growth society and the
project for a degrowth society, as well as the kind of political strategy and
issues against the present regime. Bataille cannot be a simple piece of the
degrowth mosaic. As we have provocatively mentioned in the opening of this
chapter, the degrowth thought has to respond to the problem of abundance,
not to scarcity. This means relearning how to waste, not how to reduce and
to recycle. Bataille allows us to discover some aporias of degrowth thinking
that do not only risk making it ineffective, but even to make it consubstantial
with growth society.

By evoking the insufficiency of the environmental resources necessary to
sustain the present lifestyle, degrowth theory operates a fatal reversal of the
basic problem of our growth societies. In this sense, the degrowth narrative
transfers the servile posture typical of the separated singularity to the systemic
level: thus, humanity as a whole becomes a "needs' holder," framed by the
utilitarian logic of mere survival. The point of view of the "particular existence," which emphasizes the resources insufficiency, is applied to the "general
existence." In this way, degrowth contributes to revive the basic postulate of
classical economics, that is to say the principle of scarcity. In a specular way
to the myth of growth, the degrowth project restores the state of urgency for
life that generated the glorious epic of modernity, so that it becomes legitimate, if not indispensable, to allocate all the circulating energy for the sake of

preserving the world and its inhabitants. And, in fact, the political project of degrowth translates in a long series of virtuous attitudes and efficiency techniques compatible with the alleged lack of available resources and energy.

Let's come back to the "proactive" side of the project, where the features of the degrowth society are outlined. In particular, the so-called agenda of the "eight Rs" (Latouche, 2007).

Looking in depth, it actually tends to hypostatize life and, in particular, modern anthropology. The type of man able to sustain similar guiding principles is undoubtedly the same at the foundation of the society of development and growth: none but the "modern man." The project of degrowth currently rests on the same anthropological infrastructure of the "growth" regime (and this circumstance makes it unsustainable in the long run).

We will say more: growth society is precisely condemned to the extent that it does not allow modern anthropology to persist. However, the path is not so linear. Our hypothesis is that the project for a degrowth society is based on a substantial internal contradiction: it leaves the modern anthropological pattern untouched, but frames it in institutional forms that cannot host it in the long term.

But even if the objectives of degrowth were likely to be achieved, preserving the imagination of our modern tradition, we would still obtain an uninhabitable world pervaded with the same anxiety that exists in the societies of growth.

Then, it is not only useful to think over the anthropological framework simply to make degrowth feasible, but also to thoroughly reassert the objectives and redefine both the reasons why we criticize the society of growth, and the nature and purposes of the proposed alternative.

The steady state (coming out of the actions: "reduce," "reuse," "recycle") aims at stopping the dynamic of unlimited growth, downshifting to a level of production that can ensure the reproducibility of renewable resources and the reduction of the exploitation of nonrenewable resources. Traditional societies are, as we know, a source of inspiration.

It would be easy to object (as indeed Latouche himself has done on other occasions) that in the alleged "traditional strategies" for harmonizing society with natural balances there is almost never anything "strategic," that is to say deliberately operated for the purpose of sustainability. Compatibility with nature is largely attributable to the low techno-economic power of these societies. The respect for Mother Nature is often accidental or, worse, arising from the atavistic fear of a grandiose, potentially fatal entity. Anyway, they are incomprehensible strategies once removed from the magical–religious background that inspires them.

Beyond that, the steady state pursued by degrowthers is to be obtained by an exercise of self-containment, not through acts of squandering compensation, as the wisdom of premodern societies, inappropriately recalled, prescribed. The great *potlach* analyzed by Mauss (1950) and reinterpreted by Bataille implements a steady state by moments of dissipation of big amounts of goods accumulated during a whole productive season. The demographic history, roughly outlined by Riesman, teaches that during premodern era the stationary population had nothing to do with self-containment, but with the compensation game between high birth rates and equally high mortality rates. The reference to traditional social patterns is therefore groundless. In their aspiration to stationariness, degrowthers preserve an anthropological structure wholly impregnated in the utilitarian logic, i.e., temperance and self-control. Reducing, reusing, recycling, etc. means perpetuating the utilitarian statute of goods and certainly not of suspending it, in order to obtain "sacred stuffs." A degrowth society should instead focus on the rejection of every controlling and unilinear logic, in order to restore the double movement: on the one hand, the full release of vital energy, on the other, reversion experiences.

The "reduction" is not a downward blow against the devil of productivism but the Trojan horse of integral rationalization, which tends to eliminate even the remaining anti-utilitarian outposts of the present time. It is necessary to reduce the "useless" productions, such as advertising or perfumes, that is to say to eliminate those few contemporary territories in which it is still possible to see some anti-utilitarian postures (beyond any business instrumentalization); it is necessary to reduce toxic productions (always in the logic of the unlimited search for well-being and health); it is necessary to eliminate unnecessary transports (perhaps by electing an authority that from above rationally plans the global routes of containers). But even when the reductive solution is applied to the field of labor and therefore promises a liberation from productivism, in reality it is presented as an opportunity to favor the "realization of citizens" in political and private life. That is to say a chance of positive self-realization corresponding to the old Fordist dream largely rejected by history. We refer to the 40/40 scheme, recalled by Bauman (1999): 40 hours spent for work and 40 hours devoted to citizenship. No revolution: only the wish for an extension of the second dimension. But the scheme has not held up to the test of history, since the really existing citizens, instead of realizing themselves and civilizing themselves, have preferred (as already several decades ago Adorno and Horkheimer (2002) denounced with disgust) the idiocy of consumption, waste, derealization, *dépense*. We can certainly scorn these practices, but in fact they are more suited to anti-utilitarianism than those activities aimed at duplicating the factory discipline required for the cultivation of healthy citizenship. Anti-utilitarians should find in these stigmatized practices the potentiality for achieving new anti-utilitarian horizons.

At the foundation of degrowthers' instances there is an anthropological constitution deeply imbued with the unilinear utilitarian logic of temperance, self-control, and rational management, despite all unjustifiable prefiguration of inebriating states of joy.

The homogeneity of degrowth to the imaginary foundations of the present regime paradoxically rises where the opposition would have shown more vividly: the dimension of values.

The catalogue of values of the degrowth society (altruism, cooperation, ludic attitude, sociality, localism, beauty, etc. as well as opposed to the specular values considered as prominent in the present regime: egoism, competition, laborism, consumerism, globalism, heteronomy, efficiency, rationalism) spelt out under "re-evaluating" is almost entirely comparable to another well-known catalogue of values: the one compiled by David Riesman (1950) in *The Lonely Crowd*, which describes the value horizon of the type of man ("other-directed") produced by the consumer society. In short, the imaginary that frames the man of degrowth is the same as that of the consumerist ideal type.

It is, in fact, the same list, the same horizon of values. It is truly surprising that the imaginary bases of the consumer society resemble so much the imaginary bases of degrowth society. This circumstance suggests a lot of reflections. First of all, we have to be aware that growth society is actually a wide and complex container: the features that Latouche thinks of as "revolutionary" are already rooted there. The revolution has already been carried out. Gino Germani (1971), in his studies on modernization, refers to Riesman's work to reaffirm that the culture of modernization does not simply focus on the values of competition, individualism, and so on. An authentic modernization prescribes the metabolization of the values of altruism, cooperation, etc. The two attitude scales are not at all opposed, but one has historically strengthened the other. On the one hand, this circumstance makes more complex the construction of a degrowth alternative, but on the other hand it could facilitate it (if appropriately redirected). It is more difficult because it means that growth societies have already introjected and nourished the "good" values for which we care, without obtaining relevant social changes. Using them as the flag for a political alternative could be a failure. On the other hand, this circumstance represents a great opportunity: because if the degrowth alternative really arises from those values, then it is possible to leverage on an already shared imaginary to undertake the path towards change. But degrowthers are far from this awareness. To avoid the risks and to seize the opportunities, a political strategy should be designed aiming at cultivating the seeds planted in social reality and bending the values towards a degrowth alternative. We must have the courage to adhere to the existing imaginary and then press on the accelerator in order to reach a completely new world.

In this regard, it is useful to recall the stigmatizing attitude shown by Latouche towards the "competitive repositioning" that some suburbs have adopted in the new global scenario. It is an issue that introduces us to the crucial point of the proposed alternative, identified with the slogan "relocalizing," that is the local democratic utopia.

Latouche ponders the numerous areas which, in the grip of globalization, gain an orbital condition from the economic point of view. They are deprived of economic autonomy. Think of southern Italy (Petrosino & Romano, 2017) or the Balkans (Romano, 2004). These areas are crossed by strong currents of heteronomy: remittances and subsidies support their lives.

Local actors embezzle the needed money without necessity to self-activate and autonomously manage their lives from an economic and social point of view. The *manna* fallen from the sky is then immediately diverted towards the shopping centers disseminated in the urban and extra-urban spaces, thus returning to the headquarters of the multinational companies. A landscape of completely passivated citizens, maintained by external entities thanks to an infernal circular game, reduced to pure enchanted consumers, deprived of culture, life, and autonomous capacity to produce, i.e., to build a bond with their environment.

Which political attitude should we take towards these realities?

Beyond the embarrassment generated by similar social orders, it is difficult not to see in these postures some forms, however perverse, of anti-utilitarianism, some ways of escaping from the productivist logic. These lives are spent in pure *dépense*. A barbarian, unqualified, aberrant *dépense*, which nevertheless contains imaginary practices and resources that can be used as springboard for an authentic anti-utilitarian spill. Moreover, it is clear that if these places were reconverted to the "good" productive economy advocated by the big international institutions (see, for instance, the measures churned out by Brussels's celestial bureaucracy) they would fall into a state of deep socioeconomic marginality, because, due to their unbridgeable technological and structural delay, they could only host the lower added value stages of the global value chain, thus condemning themselves to the role of handmaids of the big multinational companies headquarters. In the hierarchy of the inter-national division of labor, they would become the storage areas of the dirty work delocalized by the new masters of the global economy.

The solution advocated by Latouche is certainly not the latter. But his alternative is no longer exciting. In the slogan "re-localizing," a return to Saint-Simonianism is implied. "Real production" is the only allowed and acknowledged dimension, despite any symbolic difference and any joyful speculative artifice, so that each community takes on the whole burden of its own livelihood, by self-producing all kinds of necessary goods (Latouche, 2007, p. 33). An autarchy achieved even at the level of the municipality, which, as all economies of this kind, would end up by asking its own members (beyond any initial good wish) a work-centered overcommitment without any respite and/or a desperate status of deprivation.

However frightening, human misery has never taken hold of societies to such an extent that the preoccupation with conservation prevails, giving to economic production an appearance of finality and prevailing on unproduc-tive *dépense* (Bataille, 2003, p. 47).

Autonomy, self-sufficiency, "relying exclusively on one's own strength," control over all segments of social and economic life are typical modern aspirations. They represent the will to root the imaginary pattern of the (lost) modernity into every place. In this sense, the accusation that Latouche addresses to local development doctrine, i.e., to be nothing more than an "other-directed localism" (a formulation we fully agree upon), sounds rather as a self-accusation. The reference, from the point of view of values, is always the same: the independent man, a proactive one, who can look after himself, who needs no one. Here the will is to root the "Robinson Crusoe" model in any place: a model that is actually reported in the sociology of literature as the foundation narrative of modernity.

The local political utopia raises several perplexities. We can also imagine finding, under the alienated crust of global flows, some territories spontaneously gifted with the harmony yearned by Panikkar (1995) in his idea of "bioregion." But this wouldn't be the only problem. Democracy, in fact, is not a universal concept.[4] It is not a neutral dress that can cover any sociocultural body. Real democracy structurally undermines any inherited symbolic and cultural enframing (Deriu, 2012). And vice versa, most of known cultural traditions reveal a deeply a-democratic constitution (if not anti-democratic).

This highlights a basic contradiction: the local utopia at the center of the degrowth proposal is unbearable to the same idea of democracy that it purports to be based upon. If the demon of democratic autonomy were to be unleashed, it is an illusion to think that it would be possible to confine it within any natural limits (territorial, moral, or even "thematic"). For example, why would the territorial units remain within the size suggested by degrowthers (30,000 people)? Why, if they live in a democratic community, could people not choose to go beyond this threshold? Who would have the power to sanction any overrunning? Obviously, the localization proposal makes sense only if the free movement of persons between the local communities was to be drastically reduced; otherwise the sociocultural holism needed for self-production and personalization would not make sense. But why should a free citizen, residing in an increasingly democratic arena, choose to stay put in one's own community instead of, as it is reasonable, prefer to move discovering other places and other people?

The contradiction is even more glaring if one looks at the underlying social values of the degrowth proposal. See, for example, the call for "ecological democracy" which is always mentioned in one, and the same, breath with degrowth. The intent to attach adjectives to the word "democracy" is wishful thinking similar to the exercise of attaching adjectives to "development" ("sustainable," "autonomous," "social," etc.). Why would a democratic and independent community always choose the highest standards of ecological protection at the expense of other objectives that it could deem as more important? Who would sanction the betrayal of the ecological values? Who would ensure that citizens comply with a culture of sobriety, prefer small shops to shopping centers, small buildings to skyscrapers, and all the rest? (Cochet & Sinaï, 2003)

Degrowth advocates claim that a given political and territorial architecture (the localist one) necessarily generates a specific political agenda, one for a direct (ecological) democracy (Romano, 2012). I argue instead that we delude ourselves if we think that once a community is empowered and democratized, it will land voluntarily onto the "good" values of sobriety, *phronesis*, "small is beautiful," and so on. This is an "ontology of spontaneity" which reappears in several versions of degrowth. As in the myth of the *bon sauvage* by Rousseau, the assumption is that "letting men be," in a regime of perfect democratic immanence, they will always pursue the "good" and the "fair." Ergo, any tendency to deterioration can be exclusively attributed to the influence of vulgar or evil "powers" to be annihilated. And while there are no formidable trajectories that could confirm the reliability of this onto-logy, there is a "really existing localism" that has so far produced a lot of night patrols against immigrants and prostitutes, as well as various episodes of setting fire to gypsies' campsites, in order to ensure the hygiene of "lovely communities."

In short, if our project is indeed one of a real, radical democracy, we should not then complain if the process leads to the loss of a "shared vision," an irrationality of exchanges, or an incompatibility of production processes with environmental balances and so on. If the institutional framework of a democratic mentality is to really have a primacy over any value constraint, then the perverse effects it generates are not a "betrayal of its origins" but its perfect fulfillment. Degrowth cannot be the foundation for a project of real democracy for the same reason that "growth" cannot be the foundation. Both are "proposals" that can get lost together with the thousands of options that make up the melting pot of a democratic regime. Growth and degrowth, in this sense, lie in the same paradigm of the autonomous subject: their validity is tied to historical contingencies and none can claim the throne of constitu-tional dogma.

I conclude therefore that degrowth cannot foster a democratic order; if anything, it threats democracy. And vice versa, within a democratic frame-work one cannot take for granted that degrowth will become a value to be pursued.

The "re-location" espoused by Latouche seems to be dangerously similar to the historical process of affirmation of the "western city," as analyzed by Max Weber (1927, pp. 351–376). The foundation moment of the city matches with an act of breaking away from the centers of imperial power. The city communities endow themselves with independent institutions and, at the same time, start to work for economic self-sufficiency, producing by themselves all the necessary goods that meet the needs of the community (a necessary undertaking, since the interruption of the flow of resources redis-tributed by bureaucracy at the central level must be made up for). At the same time, an offensive is launched against any encroaching feudal and cor-porative influence: the immanence of the territorial community against the transcendence of empire!

What can we infer? That the institutional ingredients at the basis of degrowth are the same that have historically given birth to Western moderni-zation: growth, development, omni-marketization – in short, to the world against which we intend to fight. We are thus facing the old game that pro-poses the "good" modernity of the origins as a therapy for the present "bad" modernity, which really exists. What makes us confident that the same institutional and imaginary structure can produce a different outcome?

But further thought should be given to the issue of the unsustainability of degrowth society when framed on the anthropological pillars of modernity. Paraphrasing Arendt, Latouche has often maintained that "there is nothing worse than a growth-led society, without growth" (2007, p. 97). Well, with a further paraphrase we argue that "there is nothing worse than a society based on the search for meaning, which loses every meaning."

The degrowth society is certainly based upon the attempt to recover a collective sense, since it lies on the idea of a transparent, immanent, autonomous, and conscious being doing its utmost for itself and the social good. This posture, freed from any transcendent drive, exposes the individual to a continuous search for meaning. In a growth society, contemplating the meaning-of-life question is delayed due to the resorption of man in the growth adventure, which finds the existential and philosophical justification in the desire drive, as proposed inter alia by Hobbes, when, in *The Leviathan*, he argues that happiness is nothing other than the continuous jump of the desire from one object to another. Another removal instrument is *dépense*, whose practices, as we have already noted, in our society are now mainly consumed in the private domains. These elusive strategies are undoubtedly inadequate, but serve to divert the human gaze from the emptiness of life unveiled by the anthropological order of modernity. Degrowthers continue to bet on the same anthropological framework but export it to a context of steadiness of the productive engagement and of the desiring compulsion. Hobbes's suggestion for happiness is clear enough, but that propounded by degrowth supporters risks being depressive. In a degrowth society, it is generally thought we will be stranded on the edge of a meaninglessness abyss, as Durkheim (1960) suggests.

This is implicitly acknowledged by Latouche when he evokes the need for "re-enchantment" (2007, 2019; Maffesoli, 2004, 2007). But this acknowledgement does not lead to an adequate thematization. It only shows an opportunity through which Latouche reaffirms his own belief that life is sufficient in itself, that one can simply be in life for life's sake. The re-enchantment comes to being, then, a mere contemplation of the thing in itself, with a beauty that gives itself spontaneously and which alone (or maybe with the help of a skillful creative expert) fills the vacuum.

Trusting in poets' and artists' performances in order to discover the meaning of life is an excessive claim, to put it mildly. They rather have helped us discover the emptiness and meaninglessness that devour us. Anyway, the chance to remain comfortable in the convivial and creative immanence is only given to celestial figures, grown like a Nietzschean superman. Who cares for a community of mortals?

The truth is that enchantment is incompatible with the autonomous–democratic character of the society of degrowth. The truth is that Latouche fights for an ever less enchanted, more aware, responsible, and wise man.

Conversely, we need to take enchantment seriously. As immobilization, as liberation from thought ("de-thinking"). It is the only way out for the one who, once the way of unveiling has been undertaken, finally finds himself in front of the meaninglessness, and in the impossibility to employ his own living energy. The growth route is by now impassable. We delude ourselves if we hope to cross it again, but in fact we abandoned it long ago, taking refuge in private, though unsatisfactory, *dépense* experiences. Growth is no longer sufficient to free us from thought: we must acknowledge it and move on to new strategies.

The alternative of degrowth is therefore necessary, but in its present form it would be a remedy worse than the disease. Inasmuch as restoring an anthropology of unveiling (Romano, 2008) it would produce nothing but the exposure of man to the absolute immanence of life. That is to say, to its meaninglessness. It would leave energy suspended and without employment possibilities (neither useful nor dis-useful).

A degrowth alternative should instead dare towards re-enchantment. For this purpose, the concept of degrowth must be radically diseconomized.

It is necessary to reinterpret the degrowth path, first and foremost, as a reversal of the fixity produced by the regime of "universal equivalence" (Baudrillard, 2001), as an inversion of the unilinear route of promotion and enhancement of the living. That is, the opposite of the increased awareness claimed by degrowthers. In this sense, it is necessary to bring back *dépense* in the collective arena, focusing on the question of power, that is to say, on the construction of a transcendent entity able to manage *dépense* (maybe drawing on the really existing expenditure practices). A new institutional form that, far from threatening democracy, would contribute to revitalizing it, entrusting to it the creation and the realization of political goals suitable to intimately involving the community members.

This is not a radical or esoteric alternative. We have only to go back to the classics. For example, to that "charismatic power" which according to Weber has the ability to stop the logic of the selfish and utilitarian interest, to which the immanentism of unveiling anthropology necessarily leads. It has the ability to create a community and to trace a common destiny, freeing the individual from the pincer of the "infinite emptiness of all." We have to go back to Durkheim (1960), who underlines the need to control the "vertigo of meaning." That is to say, to enclose in the coffer of the sacred a series of fundamental precepts for social cohesion, thus removing them from the anni-hilating sieve of conscience, of omnivorous reason, of deliberative protagonism.

We need a power to be entrusted with the periodic requisition of the social production (widely understood, in material and symbolic terms) for its participated destruction, collectively operated: public institutions have to take a conspicuous share of the social production away from the utilitarian logic in order to sacralize it. We need this to redevelop and re-socialize *dépense*, within the framework of a new "anti-productivist communism," which on the one hand ensures people life by protecting individuals from the market and from the rigors of self-production, and on the other dissipates the excess energy, preventing the meaninglessness from spreading.

The current degrowthers claim to give primacy to other human dimensions, more qualified and purified of the growth myth, is not at all credible, because it is always subordinate to the "servile" goal of survival. The obsession for life reproduction allows, as always, to get rid of thinking, thus evading the issue of life meaning, the distressful call to be sovereign, coming from the pending and not disposed surplus energy that characterizes Western societies.

The perspective of life for life's sake (implied in the degrowth alternative) risks to be even more damaging than the one implied in the growth for growth's sake principle. In the latter, at least, man is freed from thought. He is totally absorbed by the survival urgency. In the logic of life for life's sake, on the contrary, the tendency to growth is abandoned and the human being finds himself defenseless before the surplus energy, with all its charge of anguish.

Invoking the insufficiency of natural resources to support the current lifestyle, degrowth theory (involuntarily) accepts the image provided by growth advocates of a social system haunted by a new resources penury (although rearticulated according to the environmentalist code), that consistently claims the adoption of servile strategies. Instead of working to give back the lost *aura* to *dépense*, bringing it back to the collective arena and wresting it from the cramped privatization and functionalization (as simple escapism from the productive effort), degrowthers end up participating in the servile task of survival.

This perspective doesn't allow us to identify the real general origin of modern man's discontent, so as to really understand the most decisive challenge we face. Discontent is not given by the depletion of resources, but, rather by the hypostatization of the social system deprived of any sense. It is given by an energy surplus that builds up in the "general existence" and is not destroyed by sovereign acts. The problem, we may say, is the lack of catastrophes, not their impending occurrence.

Notes

1 In the Bataillian narrative it is possible to hear the echo of Vladimir Vernadskij thinking, who in the late 1920s exercised a certain influence in France. The Russian geochemist was convinced that thanks to science and technology (that is to say thanks to the taking over of noosphere on biosphere) the human species would soon have known a phase of autotrophic development: like some plants and bacteria, man would be eating air and solar energy, doing away with the consumption of other living beings. This opened up new scenarios for his ability to forge his own destiny, definitively freeing himself from the servile dimension. The general economy of Bataille appears better decipherable in the light of this futuristic framework.

2 We clearly refer here to the Durkheimian notion of the sacred, as a place inaccessible to man, where the fundamental precepts giving order to society are preserved (Durkheim, 1960).
3 Here lies the root of Bataillian heterology (Bataille, 2015).
4 Latouche polemically objected to his MAUSS's comrades, mainly to Alain Caillé, that democracy was not a universal tool. It is very surprising that he overlooked this objection.

4 Beyond the servile

The society of degrowth

It is time to abandon the civilized world and its light. It's too late to be reasonable and educated – this has led us to a charmless life. Secretly or not, it is necessary to become completely different or to stop being.

(Georges Bataille)

Where does Bataille lead us?

Bataillian perspective, while fruitful, leaves many questions open and, above all, does not immediately translate into a concrete political horizon. It rather leads to a kind of apathy state. Bataille's narrative is marked by ambiguity and it appears as a path with no exit.

On the theoretical level, aporias are evident. Bataille constantly denounces the condition of separateness (from the totality) imposed by the growth society individualization regime. This condition nails man to the goal of his own survival and therefore to nonsense. However, meeting totality – if that's even possible – means nothing more than gaining the quiet of the matter. In short: out of totality, man is in non-sense. Within totality, he meets death. This is the outcome of the intimacy with nature. There is no way out. Sovereignty burns out in a "miraculous instant," in a loss without return.

The relationship between man and nature (or animality) is also ambiguous. The man who merely serves the biological reproduction of the living is not human. At the same time, Bataille seems to be arguing, the man who does not accept (and who does not end up embracing) his animal nature, surrendering to nature and to his nullifying abyss, is a deluded wretch. The trajectory he traces develops as follow: it is necessary for man to escape nature in order to finally return to its belly. Is it worth making this paradoxical ride?

Humanization simply leads to the acceptance of what is: the nothingness of nature. We cannot avoid being animals, but we must strive until the end in order to avoid it, finally accepting nature "consciously" (*la conscience de soi*) and finding "intimacy" with it.

Here lies the impossible and paradoxical Bataille's "political program." We find it in the last pages of "The Accursed Share." When men reach the threshold of sovereignty, we witness the epiphany of the "conscience de soi." This notion refers to a form of pure "intimacy," where the object, the thing, in its functional substance, as a useful thing, finally disappears. Self-consciousness is therefore the awareness of nothing: a conscience without an object, without a referent, which is no longer aware of something really existing. It affirms itself as an entity purely opposed to the thing. This absolute lucidity – Bataille prophesies – will be the highest form of the sacred. And it will coincide with a state of apathy.

It is clear that this ascetical perspective is way out of ordinary people's league. And maybe it is not even desirable. Anyway, this does not prevent us from thinking of, through Bataille and thanks to Bataille, a way out of the growth society. A way out from the servile logic.

For these ends, we have to completely rethink:

1   the institutional framework of degrowth;
2   the political strategy aimed at rooting it in present times;
3   its anthropological framework.

From values to form: the institutions of degrowth

The project for a degrowth society is a paradigmatic example of the "structural" inability of the current critical thought to counteract neoliberalism and to profit from its crisis. Our thesis is that degrowth proves to be ineffective (on the intellectual and political point of view), because, beyond the competition on "values," it rests on the same "form" that frames the growth regime. A shift towards degrowth is unlikely if we do not radically rethink the formal–institutional dimension of the project.

To better frame the point, it is necessary to retrace a brief historical excursus.[1] During modernity, we have witnessed a constant hegemonic alternation between a "horizontalist" paradigm and a "verticalist" paradigm, both in social theory and in social organization. We have already introduced horizontalism in the first chapter. Here immanence becomes the privileged dimension. In general, it is believed that we can find the true meaning of a social organism by looking at its single players and the networks they interweave (Adorno, Canetti, & Gehlen, 1996). At a political level, as we have asserted, horizontalism considers a social order much more desirable insofar as it leaves out the subject "as is," promoting a process of self-revelation. The more social players are free to act and interact based upon their own preferences, the more society as a whole will be happy. Horizontality appears to be the "natural" order, more harmonious, and suited to individual moods (Benedict, 1952; Scheler, 1960; Mannheim, 1991).

But horizontality constantly contends a verticalist hegemony in the theoretical field and in the social sphere. For verticalism, the truth of a social organism, its real engine, cannot be found in the single preferences of the individual units that compose it. At an analytical level, we have to consider that individual expressions are not original: they are derived from some systemic injunctions. We mustn't look at the single parts of the system, but at the whole. Because the system is not the mere sum of its single parts, but a *sui generis* entity, which works like an organism, according to a principle of unity that we have to recognize (Durkheim, 2014). There are some "transcendental" and invisible dimensions that decisively inform the players involved in the system. The individual's truth is not in what he claims to be and to prefer, nor in his behavior. His truth lies elsewhere. The verticalist logic imagines the existence of a central intentionality placed outside the phenomenal reality, i.e., beyond human interactions as they appear to the observer. In order to understand social life, we need to locate and to decode this top-down intelligence, that underlies the whole system.

What is the political–ideological implication of this narrative? Society as it is, in its immanent dimension – as it appears to the naked eye – does not correspond to its real essence. Furthermore, it is not the "right" society. The result of the interaction between single molecules is not the best social condition attainable, ergo we need to build a different institutional device that can change things from the top. Ratifying spontaneous interactions means ratifying "injustice," the law of the strongest. The form generated by spontaneous relationships is not necessarily good, nor the best attainable, as it is affected by invisible powers, behind which lurk the interests of the strongest people. We need to create instruments in order to deliberately forge the general framework of society, because its spontaneous building from grassroots is neither right nor desirable for the social players. Political institutions must "design" reality, adapting it to some selected values and principles of justice.

During modernity a sort of "crisscross alternation law" between social regulation and thought prevailed. We know well that talking about "laws" in the social sciences is always a hazard. Our claim has to be understood as a merely working hypothesis, drawn by the historical observation of the evolution of modernity: when the social regulation is based on a horizontal model, we witness a general restructuring of social thought around a verticalist axis (moreover this trait extends to social culture and imagery). And vice versa: when verticalism prevails in the structure of society, social and political thought embraces horizontalism. So, thought goes on in opposition to the existing frame.

According to Mannheim (1991), this can be interpreted as a general dynamic:

> every age allows to arise (in differently located social groups) those ideas and values in which are contained in condensed form the unrealized and unfulfilled tendencies which represent the needs of each age. These intellectual elements then become the explosive material for bursting the limits of the existing order. The existing order gives birth to utopias

which in turn break the bond of the existing order, leaving it free to develop in the direction of the next order of existence.

(p. 179)

But the mismatch between social thought and social regulation particularly affects modernity, mainly due to the specific intellectual condition that here develops and that frees intellectuals from the traditional function of maintaining order, to which professional thinkers were assigned in the preceding epochs:

> One of the most impressive facts about modern life is that in it, unlike preceding cultures, intellectual activity is not carried on exclusively by a socially rigidly defined class, such as priesthood, but rather by a social stratum which is to a large degree unattached to any social class and which is recruited from an increasingly inclusive area of social life.
>
> (Mannheim, 1991, p. 139)

These outlandish individuals provide the chance to compare with an external top-down view. They provide a reserve of self-consciousness for exploring the nature of the social system and its working model. The freedom of intellectuals ensures that thought, in modern society, is not exclusively used for maintaining order: its development is released from the social structure and, if necessary, goes the opposite way.

According to Eisenstadt (1992), this specific attitude is linked to the strong development, inherent to modernity, of the consciousness of the arbitrariness of any social and cultural construction, i.e., "the consciousness that any given order is only one of several, perhaps many, possible alternatives, including the possibility of living beyond any social order whatsoever" (pp. 68–69).

Reflecting on the faults and critical issues of the existing model, intellectuals exalt the opposite form of society. So, when the institutional form takes a top-down orientation, then intellectuals begin to exalt the virtues of laissez-faire, laissez-passer. Reflecting on the knotty problems of the existing model, they invariably uphold to the opposite, reversed form. This lag, this oppositional dynamic between theory and institutions has proven very useful in moments of crisis. By focusing on the failings of the current model and simulating its development, theorists have been able to forecast the dire consequences of a given institutional order.

In this key, i.e., looking specifically at the shifts in social regulation, we can reconsider the main phases of Western modernity.

From 1815 to 1929, according to Polanyi (2001) and as we have already seen in Chapter 1, the logic of self-regulating market frames socioeconomic life. But we have to distinguish, as far as possible, the political seasons from the regulative ones. Eighteen-fifteen coincides also with the beginning of a political phase of "restoration," impregnated by anti-Enlightenment spirit, marked by the capitulation of Napoleon, the Vienna Congress, and the Holy Alliance. However, the restoration element appears in hindsight as a consoling reaction to the fury of the times. The regulative plan witnesses, on the contrary, the affirmation and the development of the institutional injunctions promoted by the French Revolution that find their disruptive manifestation in the Industrial Revolution. We can say that, paradoxically, the political Restoration has played as the best casing of the regime against which it pretended to stand. Beyond any symbolic and political content:

> nineteenth-century civilization rested on four institutions. The first was the balance of power system which for a century prevented the occurrence of any long and devastating war between the Great Powers. The second was the international gold standard which symbolized a unique organization of world economy. The third was the self-regulating market which produced an unheard-of material welfare. The fourth was the liberal state.... But the fount and matrix of the system was the self-regulating market. It was this innovation which gave rise to a specific civilization.
>
> (Polanyi, 2001, p. 3)

The ruling pattern embodies the instances sparked by the French and American revolutions, translated into a constant loosening of the premodern communities and institutional bonds. Weber (1927, 1947, 1968), Marx (1909, 1964, 1990, 1998), Polanyi (2001), Elias (1969), etc. interpret this passage as the progressive liberation of the "elementary particles" of society (labor and land, first of all), once grouped around the castle, the belfry, and corporations. The horizontalist logic of market exchange spreads all over the West, becoming dominant and producing an extraordinary development of the productive forces. It is necessary to underline that horizontalism has not to be intended has a mere erasing of any institutional (vertical) regulation. On the contrary, the liberation of the "elementary particles" of society requires a complex macro-institutional setting. Horizontal institutions stage the conditions for the self-management of economic actors and, more generally, for the release of the factors of production (labor, land, and money); vertical institutions, on the contrary, drive the economic actors and the factors of production on the basis of a central intentionality.

In the same period, thought proceeds in the opposite direction. The birth of scientific sociology itself can be reinterpreted as a verticalist reaction to market expansion. This general thesis has been particularly developed by Robert Nisbet (1996). The 19th century is crossed (like every period of time in Western modernity) by a wide variety of schools of thought. Liberalism, for example, continues to stand as one of the main ideologies of the time, "mirroring" the institutional form of self-regulating market. "Radicalism" also occupies a remarkable place in the thought landscape of the century: it vibrantly contests the fateful aftermaths of the self-regulating market, but it maintains a devotion to horizontalism, or better to its ideal imprint. Nevertheless, beyond the persistence of the "mirroring" attitude represented by liberalism and the illusive leap forward made by radicalism, thought and spirit of the age are markedly oriented towards the reversal of the dominant institutions basic form (i.e., horizontalism).

> Instead of the Age of Reason's cherished natural order, it is now the institutional order – community, kinship, social class – that forms the point of departure for social philosophers as widely separated in their views as Coleridge, Marx, and Tocqueville.
>
> (Nisbet, 1996, p. 9)

The dramatic transformations produced by the Industrial Revolution, mainly regarding the condition of labor, land share, rural impoverishment, chaotic urbanization, the factory system, technology, etc., stimulate a strong interest towards social topics and, at the same time, a deep questioning of the foundations of the new horizontalist regime. The reaction spreads in all cultural expressions, from literature to philosophy, from theology to historical studies: the image of a good society is identified with the ties of community. But, in particular, the reversal mood in thought response will be progressively embodied and structured in a new field of scientific knowledge: the one called "sociology." Nisbet (1996) renames the period between 1830 and 1900 "the golden age of sociology" (p. 315).

The founding fathers of sociology question the tenets of horizontalism, both from a theoretical point of view (against the emphasis on individuals imposed by market institutions, they claim that the real meaning of social life can only be understood by looking at society from the top, as a whole) and from the political point of view (a suitable and rightful functioning of society requires to go beyond the spontaneous result of interaction, by entrusting to a cockpit the "vertical" regulation of society). But, first, they denounce the perverse effects of horizontalism on social ties, values, and order. While horizontalism spreads on social regulation, thought tries to discover the recipe for what keeps society together. How is social order born and how can we make it last? When and why is it undermined? How can we restore it? With the liberation of elementary particles of society, order becomes a scarce resource, so a new science arises, which studies its production and reproduction.

It is almost impossible to "scientifically" demonstrate that vertical thinking was hegemonic in the 19th century (maybe liberalism and radicalism were more vivid for the inhabitants of the age). What we can say, following Nisbet, is that the flowers of thought that have lasted over time and that have been remembered by the succeeding generations show a markedly verticalist trait. Moreover, it is undeniable that this kind of thought has inspired the regulatory shift that occurred at the beginning of the 20th century.

With the Wall Street crisis of 1929, the chickens came home to roost: it represented the most vivid symbolic closing date of the self-regulating market regime (although Polanyi believes that the end of the gold standard in 1933 is the real closing event). The following Great Depression is contrasted by what Polanyi (2001) calls the "self-defense of society," that in the medium run gave birth to a great transformation whose deep meaning coincides with the reinstatement of sovereign public institutions in the management of the three main productive factors: labor (social legislation), land (agrarian protectionism), and capital (the institution of central banks).

Verticalism took over – i.e., the State became the main force for social development – between 1930 and 1980. The hegemony of market exchange was replaced by a logic of redistribution. The new order branched out into diverse political forms (fascism, communism, social democracy, etc.) but it stabilized after World War II with the spread of "societal capitalism" (Magatti, 2009), where a solid alliance is reached between labor and capital: the "visible hand" of the State exerts a strong power on the market. This era too will see an extraordinary economic growth (*"les trente glorieuses"* as the French call it), accompanied by an unprecedented social development due to the welfare state redistribution strategy. Public institutions will give a "big push" to general wealth and rights.

From our specific point of view, the season that in Western countries goes from the 1930s until the dawn of the 1980s has a common character, a fundamental unity and homogeneity. But from the point of view of historical development this is not evident. The literature about the topic recognizes in World War II a fundamental watershed and it interprets the postwar regimes as the natural opposite of the sociopolitical regimes that had arisen between the two wars. In the light of the institutional form, instead, we believe that between the two periods furrowed by the war there is a substantial continuity, identifiable with the vertical principle: production and reproduction of society are entrusted to the central management of the State. We are fully aware that this way of looking submits phenomena to an extraordinary compression. We know well that it doesn't allow us, for example, to register the minimum dichotomy between authoritarianism and democracy that is a fundamental distinction in the political science. We know well that from the point of view of those who have placed the flesh of their existence on the fire of those tragic seasons this compression sounds totally meaningless, when not outrageous. We know well that many Western postwar regimes have articulated their own constitutional foundation in explicit antithesis to the prewar regimes (e.g., the anti-fascist inspiration on which the Italian Republican Constitution is based). But from the point of view of the forms of regulation, these 50 years are characterized, seamlessly, by entrusting the process of social reproduction to a central and vertical intentionality.

With the spread of this new verticalist, well-ordered, and stabilized age, the constantly restless social theorists left the scene in search of disorder. They put aside the binoculars adopted by their predecessors and started using a microscope in order to discover the strategies of individuals, their fundamental role in transforming order. It is the dawn of the micro-sociology age

(Munch & Smelser, 1992). In unison, they unmask the pretensions of analytical verticalism: now, for understanding society we have to start from individuals, from agency. Furthermore, they vibrantly denounce the risks included in the pretension of public institutions to limit and guide social action, calling for neutral governance. This mood also involves social imagery and social movements. A staunch criticism of any idea of identity, unity, and order spreads everywhere, stigmatizing any attempt to give rules to the world. A disciplinary revolt (symbolized by 1968 youth uprisings) overturns vertical institutions.

As we have underlined in the previous paragraph, it doesn't mean that the whole thought of the age was marked by one and only trait ("horizontal," in this case). On the contrary, a strong thought stream was aligned to the dominant institutional pattern, mirroring and reproducing its form. If we look at sociology, for example, the structural-functional school was almost "embedded" in verticalist social and political institutions. But its strength at the time revealed itself inversely proportional to its capacity to last over time and to inspire the future. It has shown itself to be a form of embalming of the sociological classics. As Eisenstadt (1985) asserts, the revolt against structural functionalism gave rise to a great variety of sociological schools which, despite the relevant internal differences, had in common a strong shift towards the actor for the understating of social life, i.e., a clear horizontal inspiration that has revealed to be more resistant to the burden of time.

Fordism and the welfare crisis at the end of the 1970s mark the start in all Western countries of a ruling pattern based on the stigma on public institutions and sovereign power. The self-organization principle replaces State primacy. In the economic sphere this translates into a firm return to market exchange extended to a global dimension. In the political realm we slide from government to governance. In the social domain, we witness the constant dismantling of welfare. However, the new model sees a rapid crisis. Like at the beginning of the 20th century, the commodification of productive factors (land, labor, and capital) erodes the foundations of social life. Public institutions do not have the necessary resources any longer, or the tools to organize and safeguard their citizens.

Our thesis is that the traditional game between thought and ruling patterns (the crisscross alternation law) is not working in the present crisis, started in 2008 and still raging. The horizontalist society born at the beginning of the 1980s (of the last century) is at a standstill, but a new (verticalist?) paradigm has not been prepared yet. We face a "paradigm delay."

But why this paradigm delay? And why is the "alternation law" not working in the present time?

First of all, a structural reason arises: the progressive shortening of the life cycle of social patterns, mainly due to NICT (new information and communication technologies).

As we have seen, according to our periodization, the first horizontalist pattern lasted over one century (1815–1929). The 20th-century verticalist model of regulation arose around 1930 and fell in 1980: lasting 50 years. The neoliberal pattern, i.e., neo-horizontalism, already seemed to be in crisis from 2008: not even 30 years later. The speed of the social dynamics has overtaken the speed of thought. Social theory did not have the time to detect the shadow zones of the pattern, to register its faults, its critical issues, and its knotty problems. It had even less time, starting from the critical exercise on the current pattern, to outline a new paradigm from which to imagine the profile of a new regime, overcoming the problems of the one in crisis. New technologies, mainly the digital ones, undoubtedly speed up transactions, relations, and flows. The time necessary to reach saturation mainly depends on the speed of social development, the speed of the circulating entities (men, information, money, commodities, titles, stocks, etc.). The digital revolution, the new media, the improvement of ways and means of transport make the social arena a smooth space in which relations are consumed in the space of moments (Giddens, 2000; Bauman, 2005; Sennett, 2006). The extraordinary compression of space and time, that is one of the main features of globalization, produces a very fast saturation of the development spaces.

This structural cause has an immediate sociocultural effect. The crisis of neo-horizontalism has an eminent functional, organizational, and economic nature. In other terms, neo-horizontalism finds it hard to assure "systemic integration." But despite the dysfunctions, the lifestyle connected with neo-horizontalism still exercises its full hegemony. It still inflames the imagination of people from all over the world and it streamlines their expectations of self-fulfillment, their dreams of prosperity and emancipation. It remains very attractive for the masses. So horizontalism is in a crisis on its functional side, but it is bursting with health if we look at its sociocultural side. It misfires on the level of systemic integration, but it still ensures a strong "social integration." Moreover, the trauma of the vertical regime still weighs heavily. In the shared social imagination, the memory of the State's awkward presence in social life is still vivid. And it is the object of a continually renewed stigmatization. The prospect of coming back to a verticalist regulation system – that is the only "reasonable" way – is not at all inspiring, even for those who suffer the most from the lack of systemic integration due to neo-horizontalism.

The situation we face seems derived from the beginning of the 20th century culminating with the Great Depression of 1929. We face the classical consequences of commodification of land, labor, and capital – the factors of production. The system rejects the responsibility to deal with "habitation," in favor of a blind social reproduction mechanism. Today, it is difficult to find schools of thought that explicitly claim for a real society's self-defense, for the social re-appropriation of the three fundamental factors of production, a form of verticality (Polanyi, 2001).

The current reflexive strategies – to which degrowth belongs – follow a "conformist alternative" pattern, based on a double movement. First of all, they clearly and sharply denounce the harmful effects of the current regulation pattern, on different planes (economic, political, social, ecological, and so on). These effects are nothing more than the manifestation of the classical problems of the horizontal form (Beck, 1992), but they are rather attributed to the "values" promoted by the system and not to its "form." Then, the suggested solutions, in order to face the drifts of the dominant pattern, always and invariably rank inside the horizontal form: the criticism against neoliberalism is designed starting from a horizontalist perspective and the recipes to escape the crisis, although coming from different points of view and being often reciprocally opposed, are taken from the same thought stream from which the regulation pattern in disgrace draws inspiration. In order to face the disasters of horizontalism, these critical aggregates even suggest a radicalization, although in an "anti-liberal" mood, of the horizontal regulation form, i.e., its displacement onto other dimensions of social life (from the "market" to "grassroots," for example). This radicalization and/or displacement is wrapped in the ideological ghost of a third dimension beyond the market and the State, namely the "relational" sphere (Donati, 2012). From the point of view of the dialectic between verticalism and horizontalism, this alleged third dimension is not to be found: it remains unequivocally trapped inside the horizontal plane. No paradigm shift arises.

Degrowthers' claims, in fact, recall Polanyi's typical arguments against blind growth in the 19th century. In the final analysis, they do nothing more than stigmatize the effects of horizontal deregulation, claiming for restoring human autonomy (Castoriadis, 1975; Asara et al., 2013), i.e., the primacy of people and planet needs (Muraca, 2013). When societies lose their sovereignty over the factors of production, then social, economic, and ecological disruption follows.

But, contrary to Polanyi, they do not go so far as to promote the restoration of a new vertical regime. The hegemony of horizontalism prevents this logical and natural outcome. If we look closer, degrowthers do not really reject the liberal frame of political power. They only try to reduce the destructive potentials of this system by unrealistically confining human action at the local level and by unrealistically trusting in a general change of mentality. They mostly displace the focus of their diagnosis in the domain of "values." Ecological and social disruption are not seen as the effects of the "form" of the dominant regime but more often of the prevailing myth of growth for growth's sake that rages in the socially shared imagination. So, the fight is relocated in the sphere of the imaginary: it is necessary to abandon the value of growth.

I contend that this strategy risks being ineffective, because, as we saw in the first chapter, growth is not a value in itself of our society, but to some extent the fatal outcome of the horizontal form of its institutions. It is not the outcome of a cultural investment operated by malefic powers. It derives directly from the liberation of the elementary particles decreed by horizontalism: once "disembedded" from society, individuals are naturally led to undertake the path of growth, due to the feeling of precariousness increased by isolation.

We repeat here, in this sense, Bataille's (1988) warning:

> as a rule, particular existence always risks succumbing for lack of resources. It contrasts with general existence whose resources are in excess and for which death has no meaning. From the particular point of view, the problems are posed in the first instance by a deficiency of resources. They are posed in the first instance by an excess of resources if one starts from the general point of view.
>
> (p. 39)

In a society framed by horizontality, the individualized being (or the isolated small community) is bound by the precarious nature of his existence and therefore obsessed with the problem of his survival. When isolated, he embraces a fundamentally servile position and reverts to the status of an animal, in which obtaining resources is central. The individual point of view that emphasizes the insufficiency of resources gets applied to the general collective.

One can say: why does real social change requires the changing of the institutional "forms" and not only a values change? Why do we have to assume that the effects of horizontal neoliberalism are similar to the alleged effects of the (horizontal) degrowth regime, although they are founded on very different values?

This is mainly due to a structural feature of horizontalism. As Magatti (2009) asserts, this is based on a clear separation between "functions" and "meanings." A horizontal social system – regardless of the intentions of their promoters – does not fit into a particular idea of justice. It doesn't obey any "value." It is indifferent to any principle, aiming only at ensuring that each singularity (the citizen and his networks) can freely play his game on the basis of his specific values. If horizontality is the elected form, then it is impossible to legitimize any authority that establishes specific values that everyone has to compulsorily follow. Horizontalism necessarily engenders neutralitarian institutions. So, ultimately, it is inconsistent to hope in a reform of values resting on a horizontal institutional frame, like Latouche (2007), Fotopoulos (1997), and Asara et al. (2013) do. Maybe it can work in the early stages of the system but, in the absence of a central intentionality, nothing assures that in the medium–long term all the society members will follow the same values: when the elementary particles of society are free to run, everyone runs where it wants. Horizontalism, itself, is indifferent to values (not the same for verticalism, as we will see). This "passivity" of the system towards values engenders, ultimately, ecological, social and economic deregulation. Moreover, it is the real origin of the emphasis on "growth."

As we have already noted, growth is nothing other than the translation of the modern principle of neutrality: it is "rightly" indifferent to any goal, if not to that of increasing everybody's material chances to choose and implement one's goals. After all, the principle of growth for growth's sake is equivalent to the principle of life for life's sake, in fact supported by degrowthers in their claim to protect Planet Earth from a catastrophe.

In these structural conditions, the ethical dimension is revealed to be totally harmless for the horizontal regime, which rather promotes the unlimited proliferation of values and meanings, even reciprocally antithetical. So, it is incongruous to challenge it with values. It requires that the whole citizenship adopt a certain set of values (namely those linked to the "degrowth" society): an impossible precondition.

So, we have to displace the fight for a degrowth society from values to "form," abandoning the devotion to the horizontal frame. It is the only way to attain a sovereign regime that could assure the reproduction of renewable resources and the preservation of nonrenewable resources, granting a kind of social life released from the obsession for growth. This will be impossible if we remain trapped in the political and social framework of horizontality.

Sure, the values fight has not to be abandoned. Verticalism itself is not enough. As we well know, 20th-century Western verticalist regimes have all promoted growth with great efficacy. In this sense, the shift from verticalism to horizontalism was accomplished under the same growth mark. But in the 20th century, environmental awareness was not so developed. More generally, there was no consciousness of the negative aftermaths of growth. Together with a shift towards verticality, we have to sustain the values of degrowth more and more (D'Alisa & Kallis, 2016). The vertical form without degrowth values can produce more damage than horizontalism. But, contrary to horizontalism, verticalism is not indifferent to values. If we feed the vertical form with degrowth values, we can hope to obtain a degrowth society. The opposite is not true: degrowth values inside a horizontal frame do not produce a degrowth society, for the above-mentioned reasons, i.e., because horizontalism is indifferent to any value. So we must aim at a verticalist regime framed by degrowth values.

How to root degrowth in our times?

As we've argued in Chapter 2, the strategy largely hegemonic among degrowthers for the transition towards degrowth, that coincides with the voluntary simplicity pattern, seems to us ineffective. Degrowthers bet that by staging here and now, i.e., in the horizontal dimension, concrete experiences of communitarian degrowth, people will be seduced by their "good foundation" and thus follow the example. In this way, change will spread "from below" and conquer the whole society. Degrowthers bet that it is possible to *horizontally build* (i.e., starting from themselves) *a horizontal social alternative.*

We completely disagree with this path. On the contrary, we think that: (1) we do not have to start from ourselves, i.e., from the elite (hoping that everybody will copy us) but from the feelings, the needs, the desires of the really existing people (i.e., trying to graft a degrowth alternative in the sociohistorical processes); (2) the relation between citizens and institutions must be framed in a *vertical* form in order to set up a real degrowth alternative, i.e., a "sovereign" society freed from servilism.

The reasons for the ineffectiveness of a horizontal alternative against the present horizontal (neoliberal) form of regulation have been explained above. These reasons also affect the imagined path of transition to degrowth, in so far as the alternative staged in the grassroots dimension leaves untouched the neutralitarian institutions in office and ends up in the cauldron of the countless options offered by the market of lifestyles. Hence, it represents another set of "values" that adds to the wide range of the existing "products," without challenging the neutral "form" of the general system.

Beyond this, there is an obvious problem with the horizontal building of a horizontal alternative: the need for degrowth is presented as something very urgent, but spreading it by an elitist strategy of voluntary simplicity can only be a slow process, and this is somehow acknowledged by degrowth advocates. It is inconsistent to state the absolute urgency of degrowth and then choose a path which promises to be long, difficult, and uncertain (at best) in its outcome. Of course, many degrowth authors propose these experiences of voluntary simplicity as a testing ground for a post-disaster period. Simplicity or low-carbon experiences, such as the transition towns, are advocated as survival exercises that will be copied once the anticipated catastrophe finally arrives. But, paraphrasing Keynes, "after the catastrophe we will all be dead."

Degrowth supporters and theorists do not care so much to embody and relate their arguments to actual, existing social and historical processes, i.e., to match them with the will, values, and attitudes of the existing social actors. But in our view, it is very difficult to fight the growth-for-growth's-sake regime without fully recognizing the hegemony that its imaginary has on the masses, touching on their deepest emotions and activating their dearest desires. This kind of "aristocratic ethics" which characterizes degrowth, unfortunately corrupts nowadays most of the political movements that oppose capitalism. Franco Cassano (2011) denounced it recently: in his telling metaphor, voluntary simplicity followers risk becoming just like those "twelve thousand saints" portrayed by Dostoevsky in *The Karamazov Brothers*, which contemplate their perfection, leaving the mass of ordinary people to the grand inquisitor's whims.

This is a manifestation of the recurring fault, already considered, of "critical thinking" (in this case of degrowth advocates) as opposed to what I, after others, have called radical, or more precisely "rooted" thought (Baudrillard, 1994; Maffesoli, 2004). In critical thinking, the operator of the criticism autonomously composes a set of "right" values, principles, and ideals, which then he compares with the observed reality, revealing, and thus condemning, all deviations from his idealized model. Rooted thought, instead, settles inside ongoing social processes, it catches sight of their potential evolutions and it is from there that it gives birth to its proposals of social change. The degrowth project risks being critical but not rooted. It condemns itself to dwell in a moralistic sphere, without connecting to the flesh and soul of real social actors. This argument has huge implications for the issue of the transition to a degrowth society.

Certainly, the environmental conflicts perspective is a much more "rooted" approach, but an important question is whether those who fight against the big development projects are actually fighting for degrowth. The risk in the conflicts approach is to repeat the typical error of Marxist theorists who saw in workers mobilizing against poor working conditions a fight for communism. Similarly, it is very likely that those engaged today in environmental conflicts do not really fight for a degrowth society, but they are simply moved by the impacts they suffer from development projects. It is likely that their fight is not against development but against their exclusion from the benefits of development. Relevant here are the insights of the Frankfurt School (Horkheimer & Adorno, 2002) and of Antonio Gramsci (1975), who with his concept of "passive revolution" has revealed the ability of capitalism to integrate losers in its imaginary of growth and consumption, and get them on side, ratifying and indulging their needs.

For a degrowth alternative to really impact in present times we have to reinterpret, always in the light of Bataille's general economy, a critical juncture of the recent history of the growth society: we refer to the passage, between the end of the 1970s and the beginning of the 1980s (of the last century), from the social-democratic 30 glorious years to the 30 neoliberal inglorious years.

Here the growth society's inability to respond to the surplus question clearly emerges. Bataille's general economy helps us understand the passage, as well as to show the importance of a degrowth alternative (rethought in the light of *dépense*) to the growth society.

There is a widespread misleading narrative about that period: the mainstream opinion is that the big welfare state and all the typical organizational forms of the period (political, cultural, and social institutions, Fordist factories, political parties, nuclear families, etc.) crushed the individual. Transcendental forces muffled the potential effervescence of grassroots, the forces of immanence.

It is a real, ideological narrative, that also contains a "consoling" view. It is simply useful to mask our inaptitude to live in the realm of "sovereignty."

The Bataillian general economy allows us to literally turn it upside down and show how it actually serves to mask our inability to live in what Bataille would have called the "sovereignty" realm.

The growth society based on individual mobilization, as we have reported above, had its most proper manifestation in the 19th century, i.e., in the liberal era, when society was regulated by a device of "blind improvement" (Polanyi, 2001). The commodification process, in this phase, went on to undermine the "productive factors" (money, land, labor), that is, the very bases of collective existence. Despite the extraordinary economic growth that this mechanism generated, people's lives have been profoundly endangered. The commodification of the productive factors leads, according to Polanyi, to the destruction of society. The "great transformation" engenders a radical change (always, however, within the framework of the growth society) of the human condition. By restoring a "vertical" principle in the management of society, the existence of citizens is secured. What Polanyi calls habitation is restored. The extraordinary economic growth generated by modernity is now redistributed by the structures and institutions of verticalism, such as the welfare state or the Fordist factory, the latter specifically characterized, as we know, by the inclusion of workers in the cycle of consumption of goods they themselves produce. Western citizens are no longer just mere "producers" (that is, servants), but also, to some extent, beneficiaries of well-being. They become consumers. Humanity (at least in its Western portion) believes itself emancipated from "need."

As Bataille (1988) argues, imagining the effects of the postwar development, this realization is linked to the expansion of high living standards. It is comparable to the shift from animal to man.

The institutional devices of the 30 glorious years have allowed Western people to resolve the problem of survival and so to escape from the "servile" dimension. Adopting a well-known Marxian dichotomy (Marx, 1973), welfare regimes have led man in "history": they have released man from the "pre-historical" regime of the struggle for survival, freeing him from any external and emergency determination, from the mere reproduction of life, in order to make him sovereign. They have released man from animalism, permitting his shift from *zoé* – mere biological existence – to *bios* – a qualified life, governed by a meaning and a self-designed project (Arendt, 1998).

Once "servilism" is surmounted, the human being finds himself on the threshold of sovereignty, where the fundamental problem arises: what to do with the excess energy that weighs down with its charge of anguish and that asks for an employment, a destination?

Staying in the servile dimension, we always know how to employ energy: it is totally devoted to the emergency of survival, indulging in a spontaneous tension towards the growth of the biological organism. But when we are on the threshold of sovereignty, then spontaneity proves insufficient and we have to "freely" decide on how to employ energy.

For the human being this was a condition never before heard of. Because, contrariwise to the premodern situation, the individualization process deprived the community of its major function in energy management, including the burning of excess energy by *dépense* rituals. Like premodern communities, verticalist modern society secures and protects its members' lives but, opposite to them, it doesn't provide the removal of excess energy. Man is now really free, really "sovereign."

At this time, according to Bataille (1988), a "social paralysis" occurs.

The strategy used in increasing the economic growth momentum beyond measure, in order to elude the necessity of "being," proves inadequate. Saturation is around the corner. And when in the 1970s Western societies experienced the impossibility of finding unsatisfied needs or new chances for development, then the phantom of social paralysis materialized.

Men in fact became immobilized. They simply stopped moving. Once the basis of their existence (labor, income, health, etc.) had been secured, they no longer showed adhesion to their activities. Work, first of all. They went on strike. A general and metaphysical strike. They started to abuse, to minimize the efforts and to maximize enjoyment. Intended as self-consumption, *dépense*. The dynamism, they thought of as coming from interior, self-chosen, desired resolutions, came to an end. Facing the possibility "to be," "to desire," and "to act," Western citizens have chosen to escape, to self-squander. The whole economic, social, political machine collapsed. A social paralysis.

This is the origin of the crisis of the welfare state, Fordism, and vertical regime. Mainstream acknowledged causes (the fiscal crisis of the State, the excessive rigidity of social policies compared to the complexity and the diversification of citizens' needs) are indeed "epiphenomena" (O'Connor, 2002). They are the symptoms of the *impasse*, not their causes.

So the vertical form taken by 20th-century institutions has been instrumental to the implementation of a "horizontalist ideology," proper to modernity, as such aimed at the liberation of the elementary particles of society (Parsons, 1991). Functional verticalism served the horizontal conception of life. In fact, vertical institutions generously accomplished their mission: enabling individuals to build their autonomy and to support them in the attainment of their elected goals. But the adventure only revealed the vacuum. It has led to paralysis.

In this sense, the failure of the verticalist institutions has indeed to be interpreted as the failure of the horizontalist view.

Once the threshold of sovereignty is attained, which strategy has been adopted by Western societies in order to overcome social paralysis?

In our opinion, instead of accepting the challenge of sovereignty (i.e., establishing a degrowth society, rethought in the light of the *dépense*), Western societies have chosen the opposite way, the most well-known and most comfortable shortcut: they have chosen to radicalize the "servile" frame inscribed in the emergency imprinting of the origins of modernity. They turned their backs on the possibility of a "sovereign life," artificially staging, with a back flip, a new state of emergency for citizens' survival. From another point of view, we can say that, instead of seizing the opportunity to re-build the communitarian whole, thanks to the accumulated energy surplus, Western societies have chosen to undertake a new, more radical cycle of "individualization," of separation of the individual from the collective arena. It is the strategy that we have called elsewhere of "mobilizing precarization" (Romano 2008, 2016), a policy strategy deliberately aimed at erasing social protection, to make citizens' lives precarious again, in order to re-mobilize them. Institutions are no longer called to freeing the individual from need: now, and again, the actor must self-emancipate. The goal is to transfer man, once again, in the prehistoric realm, far from humanity, qualified life, autonomy, freedom, sovereignty, so that he can return to respond to the "hyper-vertical" injunction of survival. What happened in the verticalist age shows that the sovereign man derails, stops being and acting. He self-squanders. Above all, he embraces an antisocial conduct, devoting himself to self-enjoyment and losing collective values. We have to maintain him in an animal state, under the blackmail of survival, so that he returns to obeying the social duties. Mobilizing casualization represents the restoration of one of the crucial Weberian requisites of capitalism, i.e., the "substantial obligation" for the worker to sell his labor on pain of his survival (Weber, 1927, p. 277). The welfare state has in fact eroded this obligation, thus threatening one of the foundations of the reproduction of capitalism.

Here comes the Reagan administration's motto "starve the beast!," restyled 30 years later by Steve Jobs: "stay hungry, stay foolish." A starved beast is always an obedient creature.

When sovereignty is fully delegated to individuals, then any sovereign entity, able to shape social life, is erased. This is the real meaning and function of mobilizing casualization policies. The individual is mere undifferentiated energy, without destination – as Durkheim (2014) asserted. So, in general, entrusting individualization directly to the individual is the best way to ensure that he will never individualize. Only the system, with its strength, may empower individuals. Erasing the system means structurally preventing the individual needs to be satisfied and that the individual can acquire the condition of security necessary to freely conceive and implement his life project. Without a vertical system it is impossible to imagine an equal distribution of enabling resources to the largest number of citizens.

As we have repeatedly underlined, according to Bataille the challenge of excess energy (in all its aspects, both tragic and glorious) becomes visible only if we are able to relocate our point of view at a systemic level and this is possible when we escape the servile regime (i.e., after having solved the problem of survival). At the end of the 30 glorious years, men touched the horizon of the "general existence," in the accursed realm of sovereignty.

Mobilizing casualization policies are precisely intended to dismantle the systemic level in order to remove the view of excess energy and to reject paralyzing sovereignty. Once deprived of the collective strength provided by vertical institutions, the individual can finally remove the anguish triggered by the excess energy and he can rediscover the "consoling" survival emergency. So, it is crucial to atomize the citizen, reducing him to the state of an isolated individual by abolishing social rights, de-securing his work, eliminating risks assurances, etc. Casualization is not, as it is often presented, a mere secondary effect of capitalistic restructuring, but a self-defense device adopted by the social organism itself. A new, reversed form of self-defense of society: the one considered at the time by Polanyi raised against market atomization; here the self-defense is deployed against the securing institution. Once isolated, the main concern for the subject becomes personal survival and the big problem of the excess energy finally disappears. Perpetually undertaking survival practices, the individual liberates himself from the state of paralysis when faced with the necessity of "being," which arises through the emergence of excess energy. Remaining an animal, in other words, frees him from the unsustainable fatigue of becoming human.

Postmodern man claims to have forgotten the knowledge and the institutional forms inherited by his modern predecessor, which allows the resolution of the survival issue for the whole society: he destroys – like a metaphysical Luddite – the collective machine that had permitted him to escape from the servile dimension. If the inspiring principle of the old welfare was "to give the maximum to the largest number" (Dahrendorf, 1981, p. 89), the new ruling principle is "to prevent the largest number from achieving anything," or making any achievement always impermanent, revocable and insufficient, so that the "need for achievement" (McClelland, 1961) strongly re-emerges, reactivating the desiring subject, obedient and meek at the same time.

The collective machine gives way to the domination of two main devices in the management of social activation: the market and the project (Boltanski & Chiapello, 2007).

We have often used, talking about horizontalism, the metaphor of the "elementary particles." Freeing the elementary particles, i.e., releasing the single components (individuals and their networks) from the whole to which they belong (society) is the keyword of horizontal belief. In order to better understand the strategy of mobilizing casualization that frames neo-horizontalism, we have to refer to the paradox of the electron in the elementary particle physics, recalled by Žižek (2001):

> the mass of each element in our reality is composed of its mass at rest plus the surplus generated by the acceleration of its movement; however, an electron's mass at rest is zero, its mass consists only of the surplus generated by the acceleration of its movement, as if we are dealing with nothing which acquires some deceptive substance only by magically spinning itself into an excess of itself.
>
> (p. 22)

Twentieth-century verticalism has allowed individuals (the electrons) to live at rest, solving their survival problem. In this condition, they have discovered that they have no mass, no substance. Mobilizing casualization is just intended to artificially spin individuals so that they can gain the illusion of having a mass (like the electron).

It is the same effect reported by Gehlen (1984) a few decades earlier: the depersonalization and the abstraction of collective institutions (which reach their peak in the age of techno-nihilism) foment an artificial hyper-subjectivism, without substance.

The strategy is not so rough. With the end of the 30 glorious years, decreed by industrial saturation, the excess energy is poured on the "services" sector. In this way we shift, as Baudrillard (1974) asserts, from the logic of need (which is necessarily limited by the process of satisfaction) to the "structural differentiation" pattern (an unlimited and undefined realm). In this domain, the precarious individual is called to act. The dominant ideology euphorically tells the postmodern subject: "Finally you are sovereign. You can escape the social machine and freely express your creativity." But an activity is authentically sovereign only if it is emancipated from the need, if it cuts off any functional connection with the process of social reproduction. Here, on the contrary, the creative activity is placed in a servile frame. It is needed for survival. If it is not validated by the market, then the stake is deprivation, social death. So, sovereignty is "servilized." A servile use of sovereignty is imposed.

Many authors underline that the specific character of current society (i.e., neo-horizontalism) lies in the opportunity given to the actors to freely and instantly overturn values and frames of their lives. A daily adventure with the taste of freedom. This order is variously judged: for Magatti (2009) the "sense reversibility" is unsustainable and fosters many perverse effects. For Maffesoli (2004), this is the dawning of a new and effervescent humanity of surfers on the wings of freedom. But beyond any judgment, it must be clear that this order works only having at stake the survival (of the surfer). Without casualization, surfers will stop surfing. So in the neo-horizontalist age we experience a paradoxical order in which the artificial staging of the survival emergency melds with the artificial staging of a land of opportunities to endlessly shape life, the land of more enjoyment – *plus de jouir*, according to Žižek (2008), who recovers some Lacanian intuitions.

Mobilizing casualization and private *dépense* frame the new social order.

Summarizing, the 30 glorious years led man in "history," into the realm of sovereignty. But he got to know paralysis. So, instead of daring, trying to live the condition of sovereignty, Western citizens have chosen to recover a sustainable "servile" dimension, occasionally self-indulging some "shameful belching."

Why is so important to recall this story?

Bataille's theoretical framework helps us to unveil the strong ideological foundation of neoliberalism and at the same time the weak point where it is possible to wedge degrowth as a more charming and desirable alternative: neoliberalism is a form of reply, a regressive reaction in front of the realm of sovereignty discovered thanks to the vertical institutions of modernity. The return to the "particular point of view" (Bataille, 1988, p. 39) by mobilizing casualization allows the recomposition of a picture in which the system appears as haunted by penury, so that it is again necessary to endlessly innovate and search for new ways of growth. Mainstream degrowth risks indulging this path by translating penury into a collective level, without indicating a way out from servilism, but, in fact, reconfirming the penury narrative through another split.

We have, instead, to rediscover institutional verticalism in order to completely revert the formula on which neoliberalism is based: from mobilizing casualization + private *dépense* to protective deactivation + collective *dépense*.

We have to trust and promote a change of collective awareness, like Bataille prophesied:

> If humanity, as a whole, continues to want [the principle of the limitless development of productive forces] and to regulate its value judgments on this desire, many have raised doubts about the infinite validity of this operation. We can go further, and ask the question more precisely: are the moral and political conceptions that continue to dominate our life – namely the economy – late on the facts? In our overall judgments do we not make the mistake of those Joint Chiefs that show themselves every time late on a war? In short, should not human thought follow the rapid movement of the economy? Of course, it would not be a matter of abruptly renouncing the growing goods of the globe, but the time could have come to reform our conceptions of the use of wealth.
>
> (1998, p. 278)

In order to implement a similar change, we have not only to recover institutional verticalism, but also to reframe the anthropological basis of degrowth alternative (Romano, 2009).

Homo decogitans: the anthropological frame of degrowth

Who are the subjects of the degrowth revolution?

This is a very important question for the future of the degrowth proposal. In its current formulation, degrowth works as a technical and pre-political containment device, which assumes a further expansion, if not a redoubling, of the modern subjectivity.

Degrowthers fall on the same illusion that pervades those who propose the expansion of technology to solve the problems created by technology itself, or those who wish to counteract the perverse effects of growth with further growth.

I contend that degrowth should be intended in a radical "anthropological" sense. To this aim, I propose a new foundation of degrowth upon the notion of a "degrowth of the modern subject," i.e., a degrowth of the subject that lies at the foundation of the modern notion of democracy. Such a degrowth of the importance attached to the subject is a fundamental theoretical–ideological step to defuse the *legein* paradox. It is a proposal exactly in the opposite direction to that of the amplification of the modern human subject that is claimed by most contemporary advocates of degrowth. I argue that we need to go through a degrowth of the modern subject, rather than its reflexive redoubling.

First of all, we must be aware of a major anthropological change in contemporary societies.

The ideal of the human subject that underpins modern subjectivity is very hard to keep up with: it is made for saints. Originally, it was formulated on the basis of the strong ethics typical of Protestant entrepreneurs, described by Weber (1992). This includes a hard individualization process, which requires from the subject to develop temperance and self-control, to strengthen his/her intellectual dimensions and to learn to put emotional feelings aside and restrain immanent needs and desires, in order to achieve long-term aims. The subject is expected to think of the consequences of his/her action and try to correct them before acting.

Recent social research tells us that this kind of subjectivity is declining in our times. "Nihilistic techno-capitalism" (Magatti, 2009, 2012) has fed another type of personality, a "de-modernized" subject (Romano, 2008) for which immanence is the privileged dimension of action. A person that does not need temperance or a rational mood. On the contrary, he is constantly in search of satisfaction in the short term, without remorse and without thinking about the consequences; and the new capitalism indulges in his passions, to his immediate desires.

Any political strategy that aims at grand social change, as degrowth purports to, has to deal with this sociological reality. It has to be based on this existing anthropological ground.

But, on the contrary, degrowth is premised upon the paradigm of "reflexive modernization" (Beck et al., 1994), i.e., it takes into account the perverse social and environmental effects of modernity, in order to avoid them. Reflexive modernization is rooted in the old modern pattern of subjectivity; it even requires its duplication, a squared modern subject. However, this model has already been rejected by history. Degrowth asks for its implementation for a kind of subjectivity that has disappeared from the social scene.

Hoping today and calling for a redoubling of this lost pattern, when in fact the modern subject has already kicked the bucket long ago, is not an appropriate political strategy. Thinking that proper and "wise" behaviors (those embraced by degrowthers) will spread in concentric circles in society, from the degrowthers outwards, due to their intrinsic goodness, is a gross strategic error. Cassano (2011) reminds us that the evil has the propensity to run much faster than the good, as it indulges in the most sensitive inner chords of people. The "saints," instead, get increasingly detached from the people as their example requires fortitude and sacrifice. A "saint" proposal for voluntary degrowth will never be very attractive, especially in our society, where the logic of consumption gives rise to a race for offering attractive lifestyles, regardless of their wisdom, and beyond good and evil.

Paradoxically, we must yield autonomy to gain more autonomy. It is the subject that accepts to deflate his/her own vision, the subject that could also accept and implement the vision built by the community he/she belongs to. Similarly, only a subject who accepts "to be evermore less" can also accept "to have evermore less," i.e., to undertake a degrowth path. To attain degrowth and the recovering of collective sovereignty we need to put our stakes on a new pattern of subjectivity. Developing this new subjectivity must be the primary battle for degrowthers.

So the degrowth proposal must walk on the shoulders of other subjects. It is necessary to uproot the voluntarist hegemony inside the degrowth movement and then to rebuild degrowth as a "political" alternative.

We must instead turn our eyes towards those places where at least two conditions are met: (1) the liberal frame of political power does not produce benefits for population; (2) it is possible to pick the trail of a different anthropological frame.

The Mediterranean region is relevant here, and we will focus on it shortly. But before that, the "other Africa," many times portrayed by Serge Latouche (1997, 2009), deserves a mention.

African degrowth

The only service that we can provide to the damned of the earth abiding in the South of the world (in Africa in particular) is to finally get out of their hair, not only physically, but above all – a far more arduous undertaking – on the imaginary level. After that, if we ever have a supplement of wisdom, we could even dare to transit to the second stage of the gift circuit: that is, the obligation to "receive" (after having so much "given" one way, without compensation, according to the "power handbook"). In other words, we could accept learning from Africa, from the solidarity practices that are daily staged in the vernacular society, to alleviate the social and ecological malaise that our myths of unlimited growth and progress incessantly continue to produce.

Serge Latouche (2009) clarifies once and for all that degrowth is not a perspective exclusively for rich countries, only useful to solve the environmental and social problems of the hyper-developed countries. The proposal does not coincide with the experiment of communicating vessels, for which it is necessary to decrease the First World, so that the Third World has access to its deserved ration of economic growth. What is bad for the saturated Western consumers does not become alchemically good for Africans.

Africa is actually the real place of inspiration and experimentation (already today) of the degrowth alternative. Not intended as depression, negative growth, but as the construction of a pattern dominated by another logic, in which the economic dimension is "embedded" in society, according to the well-known expression of Polanyi, in which the objective of growth for growth's sake has no place, in which social ties have primacy over the fetishism of commodities. Africa (as opposed to the West, which is seriously lagging behind) is therefore already well on the right path, the path of degrowth.

Obviously, the Africa of degrowth, mentioned by Latouche, is not the official one, monitored by statistical data collectors and, more recently, besieged by Chinese investments. It is "the other Africa" (Latouche, 1997). A subterranean Africa, invisible to our old radars, the one in which the river of people excluded from the path of mimetic development (i.e., copied by

Western models) organize themselves in order to stubbornly and miraculously continue to lead a dignified existence. This is a veritable miracle. If official data truly mirror reality, we should conclude that Africa does not exist: in fact, it represents only 2% of the world product. The existence of millions of people cannot be ensured by this little share. The figure alone indicates that Africans are elsewhere, sheltered from the official economy. In remote rural villages and slums near the big towns, the development castaways create clusters: they meld by solidaristic neo-clanic intertwining to meet the needs that the world market will never satisfy.

Latouche illustrates, in particular, the case of the Grand Yoff, a crowded district of Dakar, and he even enjoys "calculating" (ironically mimicking our obsessive accounting logic) the miracle of the vernacular society. It is not possible to go into the technical details, but the author's brilliant treatment clearly shows us how the "social divine" (as Durkheim would say) acts as an authentic multiplier of collective wealth: the 330 million CFA francs entering the Grand Yoff with the salaries that the inhabitants grasp from the city finally become 9,240 million. A very modest quantity of goods and/or money stolen from the official economy is sufficient to maintain entire clusters of "connected" people, i.e., actors kept together by wide and often completely fictitious kinship bonds, which form self-help nebulas. This becomes possible thanks to the return to the logic of gift and reciprocity, which we normally consider as relics of the past. The *"tontines"* (informal banks almost always managed by women) collect the savings of the connected people and convey it from time to time to the neediest among them, who, in due course, will share their savings to help others connected.

The vernacular society hosts several activities: from the semi-legal trafficking (drugs, used clothes, etc.) to the self-production of poor foodstuffs, craft services (blacksmiths, carpenters), etc. It is not their "economic" content that matters, but their "social" container, the dense network of neo-clanic mutual assistance ties that keep stakeholders together. Almost all scholars, international institutions, NGOs, etc. are inclined to believe that this informal nebula can be formalized: it is seen as a primordial, albeit confused, expression of the market game and from this conviction springs a plethora of policies aimed at detaching the economic substance from the social glue to relocate it in the official market. These policies are accompanied, at the macro level, by measures aimed at rejecting the whole of Africa in the international free trade arena. By citing the cases of cocoa and bananas, Latouche shows us the disastrous consequences of this operation, which is closely linked to the debt issue, whose annulment constitutes nothing more than a smokescreen.

The informal society is not the market's past, but its future. Here the social domain recovers the lost sovereignty over the lives of its members, also by original forms of democratic confrontation, such as *"palabre"* (a system of dispute resolution, in which the interested parties start long discussions ending only when an agreement is reached). This process should be politically supported. Not the marketization of reality. How?

Latouche (2009) suggests an African declination of his "eight Rs" program, in order to rebuild an autonomous society:

> Rupturing with the economic and cultural dependence on the North. Reconnecting the thread of a story interrupted by colonization, development and globalization. Re-finding and regaining their own cultural identity. Reintroducing specific products, forgotten or abandoned, and the "anti-economic" values linked to the past of these countries. Recovering traditional techniques and skills.
>
> (p. 61)

What is perhaps less convincing of the Latouchian discourse concerns the actual chances of success of African degrowth against the Western development model. Latouche operates, in this regard, an excessively reductive dichotomization: the African vernacular society would contain in itself vivacity, human warmth, relational fullness, sounds, scents, colors, emotions, etc.; while the West would still be the gray realm of rationalization, of temperance, of solitude, of quantitative fetishism, etc. If things really were this way, there would be no match: degrowth would have already won; Africans would not run away en masse every day from their countries, the towns of the First World would have no attractive properties for them, etc. The truth, however, is that the West has been able to embody many of those dimensions that give depth and meaning to human life and that Latouche considers the exclusive prerogative of the vernacular society. On this issue it would be necessary to deepen the reflection, to acknowledge the complexity of reality.

The de-thinking subject

Our major place of inspiration, in order to trace the anthropological frame of degrowth, is certainly the Mediterranean, where the "de-thinking subject" resides (Bene, 1995). Hence, our view on the Mediterranean is quite different from current "Mediterraneanism."[2]

This one describes a historically and geographically specific logic of living and coexistence that is being identified and translated into a consistent cultural, political, and even ethical framework. As a vision, it stands as a systemic alternative or, more precisely, it recovers and radicalizes the alleged "original" roots of the West, setting them against the perverse drifts of current Western civilization itself.

> What is the Mediterranean? A thousand things together. Not a landscape, but countless landscapes. Not a sea, but a succession of seas. Not a civilization, but a series of civilizations stacked on each other.... Traveling in the Mediterranean ... means meeting ancient realities, still alive, side by side with ultra-modernity.
>
> (Braudel, 1985, pp. 7–8)

This representation of the Mediterranean reality immediately inspires Mediterraneanism as a political ideal coinciding with a world in which it becomes possible for multiple cultures, even belonging to different stages of civilization, to live together copying, overlapping, affecting, and altering each other. So, before any specific cultural identity or social model, Mediterraneanism alludes first and foremost to multiplicity as a value in itself: the accidental historical coexistence of multiple ways of living in a single basin becomes the deliberate design of a political horizon of conviviality – i.e., the mutual acceptance and appreciation of differences, following a general logic by which any culture tries to draw what it lacks from the experiences carried on by other cultures. In this sense, Mediterraneanism opposes both universalism (as the discovering of a single humanity beyond any cultural crust) and communitarian nostalgia (responding with cultural seclusion to the anomic drifts of universalism).

While the Mediterranean area has been a constant subject of investigation and reflection for social scientists (historians, anthropologists, economists, sociologists, etc.), Mediterraneanism reaches its most accomplished and systematic formulation in the mid-1990s, thanks to the "meridian thinking" by the Italian philosopher and sociologist Franco Cassano (2012). Conceived within the cultural climate of postmodernism, postcolonialism, anti-utilitarianism, the book is particularly inspired by the critique of the world's Westernization proposed by Serge Latouche (1996). According to Cassano (2012), the etymology ("mediating the lands") and the physical–geographical configuration of the Mediterranean embody the meaning of meridianism. A particular complicity between land and sea is staged here. The sea is a constant presence for the people who live around the Mediterranean, together with the awareness that beyond it they will find other lands, other people, other cultures, and diverse ways of life. Land becomes a general metaphor of identity and rooting; sea, on the other hand, a metaphor of emancipation, liberty, escaping from the self and opening to the other. Each one, by itself, runs into risks: land, without the presence of the sea, will know identitarian seclusion, refusal of the other, despotism. Exclusively choosing the sea, however, might expose one to the vacuum of the ocean where all meanings are erased and all differences flattened and reduced to a universalistic abstraction, under the exclusive domain of technique. The two tendencies could be found in the biographies of Nietzsche and Heidegger. The former pushes his emancipatory adventure until losing himself in the desert of madness; the latter goes back to the land, to the identitarian seclusion of the German Black Forest. Against these two specular drifts, Mediterraneanism claims for "measure" (something connected with *phronesis*, wisdom), as the cultural attitude that allows for the coexistence of roots and emancipation, the sense of belonging and liberty, tradition and modernity, sense and sensitivity. A measure without pacification, not aspiring to a synthesis, according to the Greek rhetorical tradition of the *dissòi lógoi*, i.e., the divergent discourses that never meld with the uniqueness of modern *logos*.

Mediterraneanism interprets the spreading of religious radicalization in our times as a reply to the Western fundamentalism of growth and modernization (hubris). In order to hold at bay every form of radicalization, we have to learn from the historical experience of cohabitation in the Mediterranean (with three monotheistic religions and multiple cultures belonging to three different continents). The Homeric character of Ulysses becomes the anthropological reference model for Mediterraneanists: during his amazing circumnavigation of the Mediterranean, with its multiple worlds, Ulysses never loses the nostalgia for home, to where he finally returns. *Nostos* (the return) is thus highlighted as the key virtue. The desire to meet the Other is reconciled with the love for one's homeland.

The core principles of Mediterraneanism have proven ineffective for the design of real political alternatives to Western modernity.[3] But perhaps for these very reasons the conditions for imagining other ways of living continue to exist there: the unfitness of the Mediterranean countries to meet the current standards of economic efficiency (they cannot compete either on technological innovation or on the cost of labor for structural reasons), makes them a favorable place for experimentation of "delinking" and self-sufficient economies.

Inside this general scenario, it is possible to meet another version of Mediterraneanism, that can be grasped by evoking a specific mask of Ulysses.

In order to escape from Polyphemus, the Homeric hero invented the pseudonym "Noman." The cunning of a "disappearing identity" enabled Ulysses to experience the cyclopean world without succumbing to it, i.e., it allowed him to beat an infinitely more powerful being. This identity simulation, which may be extended to the symbolic abolition of oneself, can be found in many inner regions of the Mediterranean. The lower Adriatic (including the Italian southeast and the southwestern Balkans) is one of them.

Historically – and not just geographically – this is a very particular area, placed at the crossroads between Eastern and Western civilization, and between Northern efficiency and Southern stasis. For centuries its lands have been the extreme periphery of flourishing civilizations and grandiloquent empires, dwelling at a distance from the centers of power. This peripheral condition has produced an "anti-identitarian" construction of subjectivity, i.e., a strategy of absence. This is characterized by a double movement: on the one hand mimicry and on the other preservation of a steady logic of social reproduction.

The mimetic approach is employed by the people to gain the favor of the representatives of history, namely the colonizers in office. The lower Adriatic inhabitant has developed a special ability to wear the signs of conversion to the various historical mainstreams that cross his/her moorlands. This is the "subject of dethinking," as defined by Carmelo Bene (1995).

Mimicry and a steady (a-historical) existence seriously undermine the logic of economic exploitation mirroring a twofold strategy for livelihood: the parasitic capture of resources flows from the colonizing powers (related to mimicry) and the small-scale self-production (e.g., horticultural cultivation, harvesting of nature's wild fruits, wild animal breeding). These are not just outdated strategies; they stand out in full force in the region nowadays.

I argue therefore that in order to develop a new vision we must restart from such "de-thinking" peripheries, where residents are not involved in intensively taking care of themselves, but in surviving beyond an identitarian logic. It is there that the logic of exploitation and of self-promotion gives way to the capturing of the resources flows circulating in world economy, to dissipation and *dépense*. The possibility for radical transformation emerges where people search for self-annihilation and give space to vision.

Specifically concerning degrowth, the Mediterranean may represent today an important place for experimentation. The general crisis of Southern European countries suggest that the region becomes more and more peripheral and that it is not able to hold on the growth race. Mediterranean countries do not hold competitive advantages in the international arena. They can avoid sinking only if they form an alliance and build a different arena. First of all, this means cutting the dependence ties with global competition. The failure of the blind *teukein*, evident in the current economic crisis, opens opportunities for a return to democracy, understood as a collective construction of social life. It opens the possibility for a world where the relation between humans, and between humans and nature, will not be governed by competition but by *legein*, where the production and the re-distribution of resources will be politically ruled, taking into account environmental compatibilities and stressing paths of self-production. A world where work will be reduced to foster *dépense* activities, such as social dances, agonistic games, public debates about social life and the sense of the world, etc. In brief, a world of democracy and degrowth, where market and *teukein* will serve the community.

But it must be clear that the subjects of change are not the young people who protested in the town streets during the so-called Arab spring. They only wanted to reach the life standards of Western big society. The subjects of change are lazy people who, beyond any religious frame, express the will for protection, refusing the market anomic competition where they are losers and claiming to restore the social control over economic ties.

Such a strategy, compared to the one currently adopted by degrowth advocates, has the advantage of connecting itself more easily with contemporary social reality. The new Mediterranean space could meet the demodernizing and neo-tribal subjectivity trends that are spreading all over the world, stealing them from the clutches of techno-nihilist capitalism and from the global corporations that profit from it.

The current crisis solicits also the re-establishment of a collective control over money, labor, and nature (land), as stated by Polanyi (2001). Almost 40 years of frenzied neoliberalism and techno-nihilist capitalism have eroded the foundations of society. Those who care about creating an alternative degrowth future need to take a leading role, and put in the political arena a model of protection that places the preservation of the natural balance (and hence degrowth) at its center, as well as the self-establishment (self-institution) of society, that is, the return of collective sovereignty and of a real democracy.

This is not easy of course: first of all because, in general, the trauma from the omnipotence of the State is still too recent, as we have already noted; and, second, because, at a more specific level, the degrowth movement is still lagging in its devotion and connection with civil society and the grassroots. We have to uproot the voluntarist hegemony inside the degrowth movement and then to rebuild the degrowth alternative on a purely political stand.

De-thinking degrowth

As a rule, current horizontalism creates a potential structural mismatch between "sovereign regimes" (if any), based on pursuing (autonomously selected) extra-market values, and "servile regimes" exclusively concerned with the implementation of global economic efficacy. Apart from occasional exceptions, the latter wins. We must never forget Weber's (1992) lesson on the totalitarian character of capitalistic norms:

> The manufacturer who in the long run acts counter to these norms will be eliminated from the economic scene just as inevitably as the worker who cannot or will not adapt himself to them will be thrown into the street without a job.
>
> Thus the capitalism of today, which has come to dominate economic life, educates and selects the economic subjects which it needs through a process of economic survival of the fittest.
>
> (pp. 19–20)

A "third way" is impossible. The idea that the global arena is a neutral space in which it is possible to build social alternatives, according to self-selected values and norms is unrealistic. The global arena is a capitalistic arena: if we build alternatives, driven only by the optimism of volition and leaving the systemic coordinates untouched, the system will impose its injunctions on people.

Today we are not facing a global crisis. We are facing the crisis of "sovereign" regimes, that during the 30 glorious years tried to preserve social rights and equality despite the spontaneous grants of the market regime. In order to survive, sovereign regimes have to fence their space and protect it from global competitive flows.

We have to choose whether to remain in the animalism of competition (perpetuating servilism) or in the real sovereignty, so protecting and preserving the needed resources from the servile external assault. Vertical modernity (that has assured freedom and justice) has been always founded on protection, on the self-defense of society. This is, as Polanyi asserted, the physiology in the history of human communities, while the self-regulating market represents the exception. See, for example, the reduction of working time to eight hours a day at the beginning of the 20th century. It is clearly a protectionist act. Inside the space of the nation state, commodities can no longer contain more than eight hours per day of the work factor. An autonomous value defined by society has primacy on what the market, in its "natural" race towards efficacy, would have determined (certainly more than eight hours). It is necessary to reinforce this logic, not to abandon it. Protectionism is the basis of civilization, despite its bad reputation. The resources to have a sovereign life, beyond the growth diktat, are certainly available.

It is necessary to develop the macro-regional logic (enlarging, for example, the EU to South Mediterranean countries), but completely overturning its goal: no longer international competition, but the collective wealth of the inner populations, freed from *servilism*, respectful of the environmental balances. Today macro-regional "vertical" power is used, where it exists, to shape the available factors of production in order to better compete, to make the use of internal resources more effective, to locally attain the minimal cost required by the global market, regardless of any consideration on the wealth of people, on the idea of "good life" we want to develop. The illusion is that the more we are able to produce wealth, the more people will benefit from it and everyone will use it to implement their own idea of a good life. We remain slaves of the global market.

We have to use power, and to recover verticality, not to indulge but to escape the path of global efficacy. We have to self-repair from the competitive barbarism, in order to attain "social" and "environmental" efficacy. This is the reversal of mainstream strategy. If we don't choose this way in a progressive frame, then nationalism, populism, and religious fundamentalism – who promise protection and communitarian warmth in a regressive framework to people devastated by the fury of globalism – will certainly spread. We cannot relinquish the vertical form to the political forces claiming for nationalism, authoritarianism, and ethnic seclusion. Instead, we have to restore verticalism in a progressive key, recovering and renewing a noble tradition by which people have gifted themselves a more dignified, open, and democratic life: now we have to feed this tradition with the new instances deriving from the consciousness of the growth aftermaths, on the social and environmental plans. We have to bet on the *tertium non datur* of a high and large (also in a mere physical sense) form of protection, today incompatible with the dominant logics of social dumping.

Politics is no longer concerned with redistribution of wealth but tries only to actively contribute to attaining economic efficacy. In a well-protected space we would produce beneath the threshold of global efficacy, but autonomously and fitting people's needs. Public powers have to centralize the profits of energy resources and seize the yield on general intellect, so that citizens can enjoy them, at the same time attaining high standards of environmental and social protection. Public power has to ensure that people can work a few hours and in dignified conditions, preventing the social system from being sucked in and governed by global efficacy. Public power must stop the growth logic and watch over the maintenance of a steady state.

European and Mediterranean countries could form a civilization alliance against global barbarism. Showing the world the feasibility of this alternative will be the basis of a new internationalism, gathering the masses wounded by the witless and blind pursuit of global efficacy.

In order to implement this project we have to come back to that moment in the history of the West (the late 1970s) in which man found himself on the threshold of sovereignty. It is from there that the thought of degrowth must, in our opinion, start again. Degrowth could lead the exploration of the sovereign realm, in front of which we remained petrified 40 years ago, driven by the above-mentioned formula: protective deactivation + collective *dépense*.

We have all the cognitive, organizational, and technical means to solve the question of survival and therefore to leave the realm of the servile. Ecological balance can be adequately preserved only if men are turned away from *servilism* (that current degrowthers continue, albeit unintentionally, to support) in order to rediscover the collective dimension which would make it possible to actively dispose of the surplus energy. As degrowth supporters we should not only struggle for socially taking care of the survival issue, respecting the environmental balance, but also to recover the rituals for *dépense*, bringing them back to the ancient eminence (and thus taking them away from privatization).

Alongside, however, we have to pursue the collective creation, for all citizens, of the conditions that allow the emergence of a "self-consciousness," in the very specific meaning given by Bataille. In fact, this cannot flourish spontaneously. Thus, we need a massive investment in public education, not to build the good officials of the collective machine, but to build a kind of conscience able to tolerate a sovereign condition, to tolerate *apatie*, by long and compulsory cycles of education, where utilitarian disciplines are reduced to the minimum necessary. It means educating people about the awareness (and endurance) of nothingness, to which the destiny of energy alludes. In any case, regaining confidence with *dépense* is the necessary condition for building the future degrowth society.

Self-consciousness naturally and paradoxically rejoins "de-thinking." If, as Bataille suggests, self-consciousness is the awareness of nothing, a conscience without any "real" reference, then it coincides with de-thinking, that stops human activism and the drifts of the Anthropocene, finally gifting man with sovereignty.

Notes

1 This issue is the subject of the author's book *The Sociology of Knowledge in a Time of Crisis* (Romano, 2014).
2 Mediterraneanism was born in an academic environment. It mainly spread through the cultural debates in Southern Europe, particularly Italy and France. The

collective work entitled "the Mediterranean alternative" (Cassano & Zolo, 2007) represents an attempt to give the new *koinè* (common language) an accomplished cognitive and political form, bringing together in this debate prominent intellectuals from the two shores of the Mediterranean basin.

Mediterraneanism has not been translated into a specific political movement, but it has surely inspired many experiences of social and cultural cooperation between different civil society expressions in the Mediterranean countries. A considerable political impact of Mediterraneanism can be seen in the Mezzogiorno (southern Italy), where it has completely reformulated the terms of the Southern issue (i.e., the South's development lag), inspiring a sort of civic Renaissance translated into many experiences of local government in the last decades.

3 Mediterraneanism is nowadays in crisis. The rekindled conflicts and turbulence in the Mediterranean, after the Arab uprisings, have affected the possibility of recognizing the area as a source of inspiration for social alternatives.

Appendix

Which degrowth? A dialogue with Serge Latouche[1]

I'm late, as usual. Even today my former master will pull my ears because of my incorrigible "meridian" vices. He is waiting for me in a semi-hidden corner of a big Parisian cafe, the one reserved for his interviews. He's frequently in demand these days. Yes, because he – Serge Latouche – is now a real "star." Especially since he took the path of "degrowth," namely the horizon of joyous conviviality freed from the obsessive myth of economic growth. For my part, I never experienced that turning point. Like any good old student, I began to behave as a "temple guardian" who defends the prophet's words from any abusive diversion. I've always thought that degrowth represents an extraordinary intellectual reduction compared to the eminence of the previous Latouche, i.e., the author of *The Westernization of the World*, which dazzled me in the 1990s to the point that I moved to Paris to pursue my doctoral studies with the MAUSS (the Anti-utilitarian Movement in the Social Sciences), founded by him with Alain Caillé.

OR: Your seminars in Paris that I attended at the time of my PhD were, for me, an infinite source of new paradoxes. I was amazed, for example, to learn, through Marshall Sahlins, that the "Stone Age" was an "age of abundance" and that I, as a modern man, lived in an age of penury. To enter into the subject of our conversation, can we say that luxury was the property of Stone Age communities and that, on the contrary, our societies are founded on the struggle for survival?

SL: The Stone Age was an age of plenty, but Sahlins did not say "luxury age." Luxury and abundance are not the same. Traditionally, in economics and even in the moral sciences, there was a distinction between basic goods (without which one cannot live), comfort goods (without which one must not live), and luxury goods (without which one does not want to live). So, luxury is already an economized concept, whereas in Sahlins's vision we have very few needs, so they are very quickly satisfied. We have plenty because the needs are limited. We can say that degrowth society seeks to reconnect with abundance. Luxury is a category that discriminates. There is luxury only if there are people who do not have access to luxury commodities. We are in an ostentatious logic, *bling-bling* (as we say in France). That's the luxury industry. Sarkozy has a collection of luxury watches (Rolex with diamonds, etc.). This is very "new rich." Carla Bruni therefore brought him to cultivate a better taste, that is to real luxury, giving him an even more expensive watch, a Patek. In a television debate, Jacques Séguéla (Mitterrand's former spin doctor, now hired by Sarkozy) said that if someone at 50 is not able to afford a Rolex, that means that he failed.

Sometimes we tried to discriminate between pomp and luxury. The pomp is not necessarily expensive. Luxury is expensive by definition. It is an economized concept.

OR: Is it a condemnation without appeal or is it possible to find also in the monetarized luxury practices a trace, a memory of the old abundance? I think there is an anti-utilitarian spirit that circulates and prevails in our societies, even in its more reified expressions.

SL: We can play with words. We must re-enchant the world to build a degrowth society. It is not a society of scarcity or austerity. When Ivan Illich speaks of the joyful intoxication of voluntary sobriety, he means that we can oppose a degrowth luxury to the bourgeois, *bling-bling* luxury of President Sarkozy. Luxury can be expressed by very simple things. My friend Jean-Claude Besson-Girard lived in a rural community rather soberly, but there we always drank wine in beautiful crystal glasses. Indeed, there is nothing more distressing than drinking champagne in plastic glasses. It is an ethics of life, which cannot be reduced to necessity. Here lies a certain kind of luxury.

OR: Maybe in Africa, which is your second home, among the development castaways, one can recognize the clearer illustrations of a certain idea of abundance or luxury, if one wants.

SL: Of course. African society, despite poverty, precariousness, etc., is a society of appearance. Women in particular always have jewels, not necessarily golden, but always something very ostentatious: sophisticated hairstyles, very beautiful loincloths. In the Congo, there was even the movement of "sappers" (those who, playing with words, undermine themselves, dress well), that is to say members of the SAPE [society of ambient creators and elegant people]. There was even inside a sub-society of "craneurs" (swaggers), which wore very bright ties. They have the sense of parade, adornment, ostentation. One of my students studied the feasts of Senegal's popular milieu women: they manage to make a kind of *potlatch*, where large amounts of money circulate.

OR: And then there are also the stories of emigrants who often avoid returning to see their relatives in Africa because they cannot comply with the obligation to bring them precious gifts....

SL: This is a tragedy, because young people risk their lives to try to emigrate and to succeed in Europe.

OR: Which is the meaning of these practices?

SL: I think that's the way they nurture their humanity. A human life is not eating, drinking, and sleeping. Fighting for recognition is more important for them, even if they have to skip a meal. Appearance is more important than survival.

OR: I remain doubtful about the possibility that a degrowth society may recover the spirit of abundance. The pauperist spiral is omnipresent in the project. This is in some way already decreed by the critical scheme employed against the growth society: it contains in itself the path to follow, the social alternative. Let me explain. If you say, as you say, that "degrowth is necessary in order to avoid a tragic catastrophe," then the objective is to preserve life (life for life's sake). And in this respect, I cannot avoid remembering what you wrote, almost 25 years ago, in *The Westernization of the World*:

> The bourgeois ethics aims at eliminating death in all its forms while imposing life itself as a value.... The exaltation of biological life as a supreme value is inhuman and destroys the very meaning of existence in its thickness quality. The West, making the world disenchanted, makes terrestrial life the value par excellence.

Well, in my opinion the project of degrowth follows the same "bourgeois" approach which is here the object of your criticism. Isn't it?

SL: There is indeed a risk, but degrowth is primarily a *slogan*, a movement, and a political project that uses a certain kind of rhetoric. The main goal is to exit the growth society. Exit the software of bourgeois and capitalist society. And by this way re-opening the space to the "radical imaginary" (according to Castoriadis). But to get there, you have to educate people using what they are sensitive to. People think that the most important achievement of the West is the rise of life expectancy. They consider it as a value. When we tell them that we have to get out of growth not because it is necessary but because it is desirable, people, as Castoriadis says, are very insensitive. On the other hand, if we tell them: "in 2030 it'll be over, humanity will disappear," maybe the reaction is a fruitful shock.

OR: So, it is just a marketing strategy?

SL: It is a strategy aimed at fostering collective awareness, it is a form of pedagogy: how to engender people's reaction, how to become aware? The new software hasn't been yet imagined and discussed. We have to get out of the economy, not only imagine "another" economy. We have to get out of the logic of need, production, consumption, and so on. We have a lot of work. Certainly, I'm not interested in the logic of life for life's sake, but as we are plunged in this system, that's how we can talk to people and get them out of it.

OR: I think that this fight requires a series of alliance that have been often missed. One missed alliance is surely that between the MAUSS and

Bataille's thought. I believe that degrowth must be re-thought starting from the concept of *dépense*, because it provides a real way out of the utilitarian–functional status of things and persons. On the contrary, my impression is that degrowth is likely to translate into an almost absolute, totalitarian, and exclusive affirmation of the utilitarian spirit. I refer, in particular, to your "eight Rs" program. Well, I see in it nothing but a perpetuation of the useful substance of objects.

SL: There is a misunderstanding about the status of the "eight Rs" program. Degrowth society is not one alternative, but a matrix of alternatives. It re-opens the space to inventiveness, pluralism, and diversity. A degrowth society is not the same in sub-Saharan Africa, in Latin America, or else-where. It is the economy that has standardized the social sphere on the basis of a single frame. There will be totally different projects. All these societies, if they want to exist and to have a future, must simply obey a minimal condition, namely sustainability. Sustainability can be split into a certain number of fundamental points. That's what I tried to draw with the eight Rs: a common denominator. I do not deal with the sense of life, of death, etc. Thus, how to fill the social container is to be imagined and implemented. Starting from our society, the implementation of degrowth follows an eight-points political agenda (10 in the latest version). Working less to let everybody work, but mostly working less to live better. Changing our relationship with time. It goes against the empire of necessity.

To come back to your question, I always had a problem with Bataille. When I read him, long ago, he impressed me a lot. His thinking was challenging and gave me a shake, but no answers. He leaves one dissatis-fied. And it's a little bit the same with your writings. I inherited a polit-ical tradition according to which it is necessary to convince the masses if we want to change the world. Thus, we must have a credible project. I'm trying to follow this teaching.

OR: You claim that without a re-enchantment of the world degrowth altern-ative would not be viable. I totally agree. Nevertheless, I believe that the answer you give to this need is very weak. You appeal to poets, artists, and all the professionals of the "useless," but it's really huge to believe that one can rely on them to have a re-enchantment of the world. They are disseminated in every society and nothing happens. Finally, this topic is crucial, but the reflection on it is quite inadequate.

SL: We continue to reflect on this point. It's a collective work. Jean-Claude Besson-Girard is more sensitive than me on this topic. But here we come up against a difficulty. The world as it is today has completely sterilized this "accursed share." Poetry makes no sense, whereas elsewhere it is different. For example, I just returned from the Basque country, where there are young people who continue the tradition of improvising in verses. They meet, they organize games, contests, parties, etc. Poetry is still important in the life of villages and peasants. In the Soule, a small province of the French Basque country of about 15,000 inhabitants, there are big festivals all summer long. A village is responsible for performing a show in verses, a drama that lasts four hours. All its inhabitants work there all year long and even those who live in Paris come back every weekend to take part in the preparation. Poetry is an important dimension of life and I think that a degrowth society could and should rediscover it. Many think that there is only the religious dimension to re-enchant the world. But it's not so. Of course, we do not have turnkey solutions. We cannot re-enchant the world with a magic wand.

OR: Our reality is forged by powerful entities of a different nature. Thus, I think that whoever claims to "change the world" must face the issue of "political power": how to conquer *Herrschaft* [political leadership, rule] in order to counteract the opposing *Macht* [power]. On the contrary, I think that this issue is completely neglected by all the critical fronts of the present society. Everybody thinks that it is possible to avoid addressing the question, rather exclusively dedicating ourselves to the construction of communitarian alternatives in a molecular and immanent frame. I think this attitude, which is also typical of the degrowth movement, actually allows the big powers to continue to shape our societies without any noise.

SL: First of all, we should make no mistake about who is the enemy. Power does not coincide with the official political institutions. Two thousand transnational corporations govern the world. In the face of that, we are deprived. The storming of the Winter Palace does not work anymore, so we have to plan another strategy. We can look at Chiapas, where a degrowth society has been created here and now. The Earth's University "Ivan Illich" has been founded in San Cristobal de Chiapas. Indigenous communities completely recognize themselves in the degrowth project. In Brazil or Canada, representatives of the Indigenous movement immediately joined the project. The same thing is happening in Bolivia with Evo Morales. The problem is how to destroy Monsanto. The green parties are gaining support in Europe. We can do a lot at the local level. There are municipalities, like Barjac in France, where the mayor decided to convert the canteens to serve organic food and, as a result, he turned the whole village upside down. There is now a great democratic effervescence. Winegrowers, who are still productivists, are questioning themselves (starting from the accidents they had with pesticides).

Majid Rahnema and Jean Robert in "The Power of the Poor" take up the Spinoza concept of "potentia." The power of the poor as opposed to the established power. The system has managed to make us powerless. Rather than for the conquest of institutions, I am for the destruction of some institutions. That's why the crisis is a good chance. The failure of General Motors is the best piece of news I have heard in recent years. When Monsanto will go bankrupt, I'll offer champagne to everyone. For me, it is more important to bankrupt Monsanto than to overthrow

Sarkozy. Of course, we still have to overthrow Sarkozy, but probably for that we must make Monsanto bankrupt.

OR: I find the track you opened in your last essay ("For an autonomous society") very interesting, in *Entropia* [5(2008)]. You talk about the need to re-establish a "status" society. What is that exactly?

SL: I've been always interested in the topic and probably my African experience has something to do with it. Democracy shows a general aspiration to justice: domination, submission to any power whatsoever is unbearable. But democracy rests on a paradox: a society of equals (who are really equal) cannot work. We are always different. To get out of this paradox, which worried many people like Tocqueville, Dewey, etc., we must combine the *homo aequalis* and the *homo hierarchicus*, the contract society and the "status" society, individualism and holism which are always opposed. I think that we must conceive a kind of democratization of the status society. It works quite well in African societies, which often lack the state, where everyone is obsessed with differentiation. We, on the contrary, are looking for homogenization; nobody wants to be different from the others, we have to behave like the others. In Africa everyone strives to gain a status. What matters is that everyone has access to a status. If everybody has a status, we realize something that would seem impossible: a democracy of kings. I saw it work in several and different contexts: for example, in the academic world, when you found a research center, even before its real settlement, the first act is to elect a president, a vice-president, a treasurer, a vice-treasurer, etc. Everyone must have a status. Everyone respects the other as a status bearer. It also meets the concerns of my friend Alain Caillé on the sociology of recognition. We must conceive society not as a global village but as a plurality of millions of networks of villages. The history of Italy in the Middle Ages, as reported by Jean-Charles Leonard Sismonde de Sismondi, is very interesting in this respect: we had thousands of small republics and in each there was a flowering of artists, philosophers, political identities, etc. There were more great men in the smallest Italian republic of the Middle Ages than at present in the global village. Sometimes, of course, they were waging war, but it may be possible to find less antagonistic relations.

OR: The antagonistic dimension is nevertheless important....

SL: Yes, it is not necessary to reciprocally slaughter or beat women, as normally happens in some societies. There are other forms: a football game can suffice. It's the opposite of globalization. We must de-globalize the world. And here we meet Murray Bookchin's municipalism. Starting from the local dimension we can rethink the European building: every little local democracy (Breton, Basque, Apulian, etc.) sends its delegates (who are not professional but revocable representatives) to a European coordination meeting (because there are questions to manage in common). This would be quite different from the nation-state centrality, which leads to a superstate, top-down imposing regulations for every-body and standardizing the whole region.

OR: To paraphrase you, we do not have to pursue an alternative globaliza-tion, but an alternative "to" globalization.

SL: Yes, the move from anti-globalism to alter-globalism made me very angry. For me it was totally counterproductive. Even in the degrowth movement, many bet on a globalist, universalist project, but I remain faithful to the critique of universalism and humanism produced by my "masters" Ivan Illich, Jacques Ellul, Raimon Panikkar, and Cornelius Castoriadis.

Note

1 This dialogue was first published in French: S. Latouche & O. Romano (2010). Le défi de la décroissance. *Les cahiers Européens de l'imaginaire*, 2, pp. 62–71. Repro-duced by permission of CNRS Éditions.

Bibliography

Acemoglu, D., & Robinson, J. A. (2012). *Why nations fail?* New York: Crown.

Adorno, W. T., Canetti, E., & Gehlen, A. (1996). *Desiderio di vita: Conversazioni sulle metamorfosi dell'umano* (U. Fadini (Ed.)). Milan: Mimesis.

Alexander, S. (2013). Voluntary simplicity and the social reconstruction of law: Degrowth from the grassroots up. *Environmental Values* 22: 287–308.

Alexander S., & Gleeson, B. (2018). *Degrowth in the suburbs: A radical urban imaginary.* New York: Palgrave Macmillan.

Alexander, S., & Yacoumis, P. (2018). Degrowth, energy descent, and "low-tech" living: Potential pathways for increased resilience in times of crisis. *Journal of Cleaner Production* 197(2): 1840–1848.

Anderson, K., & Bows, A. (2011). Beyond "dangerous" climate change: Emission scenarios for a new world. *Philosophical Transactions of the Royal Society A: Mathematical, Physical and Engineering Sciences* 369(1934): 20–44.

Andreoni V., & Galmarini, S. (2013). On the increase of social capital in degrowth economy. *Procedia – Social and Behavioral Sciences* 72: 64–72.

Arendt, H. (1951). *Le origini del totalitarismo.* Milan: Edizioni di Comunità.

Arendt, H. (1958). *Vita activa: La condizione umana.* Milan: Bompiani.

Arendt, H. (1998). *The human condition.* Chicago: University of Chicago Press.

Ariès, P. (2005). *Décroissance ou barbarie.* Lyon: Golias.

Asara, V., Kallis, G., & Profumi, E. (2013). Degrowth, democracy and autonomy. *Environmental Values* 22: 217–239.

Barcellona, P. (1985). Il giuridico nella costituzione del moderno. *Problemi del Socialismo* 5: 70–110.

Barcellona, P. (1994). *Dallo stato sociale allo stato immaginario: Critica della "ragione funzionalista."* Turin: Bollati Boringhieri.

Bataille G. (1967). *La part maudite.* Paris: Éditions de Minuit.

Bataille, G. (1933). La notion de dépense. *La critique sociale.* 1(7).

Bataille, G. (1976a). L'économie à la mesure de l'univers. In *Œuvres complètes* (vol. VII). Paris: Gallimard.

Bataille, G. (1976b). La limite de l'utile. In *Œuvres complètes* (vol. VII). Paris: Gallimard.

Bataille, G. (1976c). Histoire de l'érotisme. In *Œuvres complètes* (vol. VIII). Paris: Gallimard.

Bataille, G. (1976d). La souveraineté. In *Œuvres complètes* (vol. VIII). Paris: Gallimard.

Bataille, G. (1976e). *Œuvres complètes* (vol. VIII). Paris: Gallimard.

Bataille, G. (1976f). La conjuration sacrée. In *Œuvres complètes* (vol. I). Paris: Gallimard.

Bataille, G. (1988). *The accursed share: An essay on general economy. Vol. I: Consumption.* New York: Zone Books.

Bataille, G. (1991). *L'erotismo*. Milan: SE.

Bataille, G. (1998). *Choix de lettres 1917–1962*. Paris: Gallimard.

Bataille, G. (2000). *Il limite dell'utile*. Milan: Adelphi.

Bataille, G. (2002). *L'expérience intérieure*. Paris: Gallimard.

Bataille, G. (2003). *La parte maledetta*. Turin: Bollati Boringhieri.

Bataille, G. (2009). *La sovranità*. Milan: SE.

Bataille, G. (2015). *La lettertura e il male*. Milan: SE.

Baudrillard, J. (1972). *Pour une critique de l'économie politique du signe*. Paris: Gallimard.

Baudrillard, J. (1974). *La société de consommation*. Paris: Gallimard.

Baudrillard, J. (1976). *L'échange symbolique et la mort*. Paris: Gallimard.

Baudrillard, J. (1994). *La pensée radicale*. Paris: Sens & Tonka.

Baudrillard, J. (2001). *L'esprit du terrorisme*. Paris: Galilée.

Baudrillard, J. (2002). *Power inferno*. Paris: Galilée.

Bauman, Z. (1999). *In search of politics*. Cambridge, UK: Polity.

Bauman, Z. (2005). *Liquid life*. Cambridge, UK: Polity.

Beck, U. (1992). *Risk society: Towards a new modernity*. London: Sage.

Beck, U., Giddens, A., & Lash, S. (1994). *Reflexive modernization: Politics, tradition and aesthetics in the modern social order*. Cambridge, UK: Polity.

Bell, D. (1976). *The cultural contradictions of capitalism*. London: Heinemann.

Benedict, R. (1952). *Patterns of culture*. London: Routledge & Kegan Paul.

Bentham, J. (1839). A manual of political economy. In *The works of Jeremy Bentham*. Edinburgh: William Tate.

Berland, J.-P., Bové, J., & Brune, F. et al. (2003). *Défaire le développement: Refaire le monde*. Paris: Parangon.

Bobbio, N. (1985). *Stato, governo, società. Per una teoria generale della politica*, Turin: Einaudi.

Boltanski, L., & Chiapello, É. (1999). *Le nouvel esprit du capitalisme*. Paris: Gallimard.

Boltanski, L., & Chiapello, É. (2007). *The new spirit of capitalism*. New York and London: Verso.

Bonaiuti, M. (2009). Decrescita o collasso: appunti per un'analisi sistemica della crisi. In C. Modonesi & G. Tamino (Eds.), *Bio diversità e beni comuni* (pp. 207–228). Milan: Jaca.

Bonaiuti, M. (Ed.). (2004). *Obiettivo decrescita*. Bologna: EMI.

Bonaiuti, M. (2011). *From bioeconomics to degrowth*. London: Routledge.

Bonaiuti, M. (2014). *The great transition*. London: Routledge.

Bonaiuti, M. (2018). Are we entering the age of involuntary degrowth? Promethean technologies and declining returns of innovation. *Journal of Cleaner Production* 197(2): 1800–1809.

Boonstra, W. J., & Joosse, S. (2013). The social dynamics of degrowth. *Environmental Values* 22: 171–189.

Borowy, I., & Schmelzer, M. (Eds.). (2017). *History of the future of economic growth: Historical roots of current debates on sustainable degrowth*. New York: Routledge.

Boudon, R. (1969). *Les méthodes en sociologie*. Paris: Presses Universitaires de France.

Braudel, F. (1987). *Il Mediterraneo*. Milan: Bompiani

Büchs, M., & Koch, M. (2019). Challenges for the degrowth transition: The debate about wellbeing. *Futures* 105: 155–165.

Cacciari, P. (2011). *La società dei beni comuni*. Roma: Ediesse.

Cacciari, P. (2018). *La decrescita tra passato e futuro*. Napoli: Marotta & Cafiero.

Caillé, A. (1989). *Critique de la raison utilitaire: Manifeste du MAUSS.* Paris: La Découverte.

Caillé, A. (1991). *Critica della ragione utilitaria.* Turin: Bollati Boringhieri.

Caillé, A. (1997). 30 thèses pour une gauche nouvelle et universalisable. *Revue du MAUSS* 9: 297–331.

Caillé, A. (1998). *Il terzo paradigma. Antropologia filosofica del dono.* Turin: Bollati Boringhieri.

Caillé, A. (2006). Critique de la critique anti-utilitariste critique de l'anti-utilitarisme. En réponse à Onofrio Romano. *Revue du MAUSS* 27(1): 229–239.

Carmin, J., & Agyeman, J. (2011). *Environmental inequalities beyond borders: Local perspectives on global injustices.* Cambridge, MA: MIT Press.

Cassano, F. (2011). *L'umiltà del male.* Rome: Laterza.

Cassano, F. (2012). *Southern thought and other essays on the Mediterranean.* New York: Fordham University Press

Cassano, F., & Zolo, D. (Eds.). (2007). *L'alternativa mediterranea.* Milan: Feltrinelli.

Cassiers, I., Maréchal, K., & Méda, D. (Eds.). (2017). *Post-growth economics and society.* New York: Routledge.

Castoriadis, C. (1975). *L'institutiton imaginaire de la société.* Paris: Seuil.

Castoriadis, C. (2005). *Une société à la derive: Entretiens et débats 1974–1997.* Paris: Seuil.

Cattaneo, C., D'Alisa, G., Kallis, G., & Zografos, C. (2012). Degrowth futures and democracy. *Futures* 44(6): 515–523.

Cheynet, V. (2008). *Le choc de la décroissance.* Paris: Seuil.

Cochet, Y. (2005). *Pétrole apocalypse.* Paris: Fayard.

Cochet, Y. & Sinaï A. (2003). *Sauver la terre.* Paris: Fayard

Cosme, I., Santos, R., & O'Neill, D. W. (2017). Assessing the degrowth discourse: A review and analysis of academic degrowth policy proposals. *Journal of Cleaner Production* 149: 321–334.

D'Alisa, G., Demaria, F., & Cattaneo, C. (2013). Civil and uncivil actors for a degrowth society. *Journal of Civil Society* 9(2): 212–224.

D'Alisa, G., Demaria, F., & Kallis, G. (Eds.). (2014). *Degrowth: A vocabulary for a new era.* New York: Routledge.

D'Alisa, G., & Kallis, G. (2016). A political ecology of maladaptation: Insights from a Gramscian theory of the State. *Global Environmental Change* 38: 230–242.

Dahrendorf, R. (1981). *La libertà che cambia.* Rome: Laterza.

Daly, H. (1996). *Beyond growth: The economics of sustainable development.* Boston, MA: Beacon Press.

Daly, H., & Cobb, J. (1989). *For the common good.* Boston, MA: Beacon Press.

Davey, B. (2014). *Degrowth: A vocabulary for a new era*: Review. Tipperary: Foundation for the Economics of Sustainability, www.feasta.org/2014/12/18/degrowth-a-vocabulary-for-a-new-era-review (accessed January 20, 2015).

Demaria, F., Schneider, F., Sekulova, F., & Martinez-Alier, J. (2013). What is degrowth? From an activist slogan to a social movement. *Environmental Values* 22: 191–215.

Deriu, M. (2012). Democracies with a future: Degrowth and the democratic tradition. *Futures* 44(6): 553–561.

Deriu, M. (2014). Conviviality. In G. D'Alisa et al. (Eds.), *Degrowth: A vocabulary for a new era* (pp. 79–82). New York: Routledge.

Donati, P. (2012). *Relational society: A new paradigm for social sciences.* New York: Routledge.

Durkheim, É. (1960). *Les formes élémentaire de la vie religieuse*. Paris: Presses Universitaires de France.

Durkheim, É. (2014). *The rules of sociological method: And selected texts on sociology and its method*. New York: Free Press.

Durkheim, É., & Mauss, M. (1970). *Primitive classification*. London: Cohen & West.

Dzimira, S. (2007). Décroissance et anti-utilitarisme, *Revue du Mauss permanente*, May 26. Available at www.journaldumauss.net/./?Antiutilitarisme-et-decroissance (accessed October 4, 2013).

Eisenstadt, S. N. (1976). *The form of sociology: Paradigms and crises*. New York: Wiley.

Eisenstadt, S. N. (1985). Macro-societal analysis – Background, development and indications. In S. N. Eisenstadt & H. G. Helle (Eds.), *Perspectives on sociological theory. Vol. 1. Macro-sociological theory* (pp. 7–16). London: Sage.

Eisenstadt, S. N. (1992). The order-maintaining and order-transforming dimensions of culture. In R. Münch & N. J. Smelser (Eds.), *Theory of culture* (pp. 64–87). Berkeley and Oxford: University of California Press.

Eisenstadt, S. N., &. Helle, H. J. (1985a). *Perspectives on sociological theory. Vol. 1. Macro-sociological theory*. London: Sage.

Eisenstadt, S. N., &. Helle, H. J. (1985b). *Perspectives on sociological theory. Vol. 2. Micro-sociological theory*. London: Sage.

Elias, N. (1969). *Il processo di civilizzazione*. Bologna: Il Mulino.

Elias, N. (1990). *La società degli individui*. Bologna: Il Mulino.

Fotopoulos, T. (1997). *Towards an inclusive democracy*. London: Cassell Continuum.

Foucault, M. (1976). *La volonté de savoir*. Paris: Gallimard.

Foucault, M. (2001). *Power*. London: Allen Lane.

Foucault, M. (2010). *Eterotopia*. Milan: Mimesis.

Foucault, M. (2011). *The government of self and others: Lectures at the Collège de France, 1982–1983*. Basingstoke: Palgrave Macmillan.

Freud, S. (1990). *Beyond the pleasure principle*. New York: Norton.

Fromm, E. (1994). *Fuga dalla libertà*. Milan: Bruno Mondadori.

Garcia, E., Martinez-Iglesias, M., & Kirby, P. (Eds.). (2018). *Transitioning to a post-carbon society: Degrowth, austerity and wellbeing*. New York: Palgrave Macmillan.

Georgescu-Roegen, N. (1971). *The entropy law and the economic process*. Cambridge, MA: Harvard University Press.

Georgescu-Roegen, N. (1994). *La décroissance* (Rens & J. Grinevald (Eds.)). Paris: Sang de la Terre.

Georgescu-Roegen, N. (2014). *From bioeconomics to degrowth*. New York: Routledge.

Germani, G. (1971). *Sociologia della modernizzazione*. Bari: Laterza.

Giddens, A. (2000). *Runaway world: How globalization is reshaping our lives*. London: Profile.

Gómez-Baggethun, E. (2014). Commodification. In G. D'Alisa et al. (Eds.), *Degrowth: A vocabulary for a new era* (pp. 67–70). New York: Routledge.

Gordon, R. J. (2012). Is U.S. economic growth over? Faltering innovation confronts the six headwinds. National Bureau of Economic Research Working Paper No. 18315.

Gorz, A., & Bousquet, M. (1977). *Écologie et politique*. Paris: Seuil

Gramsci, A. (1975). *Quaderni del carcere*. Turin: Einaudi.

Gunderson, R. (2018). Degrowth and other quiescent futures: Pioneering proponents of an idler society. *Journal of Cleaner Production* 198: 1574–1582.

Harvey, D. (2005). *A brief history of neoliberalism*. Oxford: Oxford University Press.

Harvey, D. (2006). *Spaces of global capitalism: Towards a theory of uneven geographical development*. New York: Verso.

Harvey, D. (2011). *The enigma of capital and the crises of capitalism*. London: Profile Books.

Hegel, G. W. F. (1976). *The phenomenology of spirit*. New York: Oxford University Press.

Heikkurinen, P., Lozanoska, J., & Tosi, P. (2019). Activities of degrowth and political change. *Journal of Cleaner Production* 211: 555–565.

Hirsch, F. (1978). *Social limits to growth*. London: Routledge.

Hobsbawm, E. J. (1994). *Age of extremes: The short twentieth century*. London: Michael Joseph.

Horkheimer, M., & Adorno, T. W. (2002). *Dialectic of enlightenment*. Stanford, CA: Stanford University Press.

Husserl, E. (2000). *The crisis of European sciences and transcendental phenomenology*. Evanston: Northwestern University Press.

Illich, I. (1972). *Deschooling society*. London: Calder & Boyars.

Illich, I. (1973). *Tools for conviviality*. New York: Harper & Row.

Illich, I. (1977). *Limits to medicine. Medical nemesis. The expropriation of health*. Harmondsworth: Penguin.

Inglehart, R. (1990). *Culture shift in advanced industrial society*. Princeton, NJ: Princeton University Press.

Inglehart, R. (1997). *Modernization and postmodernization: Cultural, economic, and political change in 43 societies*. Princeton, NJ: Princeton University Press.

Jackson, T. (2016). *Prosperity without growth*. New York: Routledge.

Kallis, G. (2011). In defence of degrowth. *Ecological Economics* 70(5): 873–880.

Kallis, G. (2013). Societal metabolism, working hours and degrowth: A comment on Sorman and Giampietro. *Journal of Cleaner Production* 38: 94–98.

Kallis, G. (2018a). *In defense of degrowth: Opinions and minifestos*. Uneven Earth Press.

Kallis, G. (2018b). *Degrowth*. Newcastle upon Tyne, UK: Agenda Publishing.

Kallis, G., Demaria, F., & D'Alisa, G. (2015). Degrowth. In J. D. Wright (Ed.-in-chief), *International Encyclopedia of the Social & Behavioral Sciences* (2nd ed.), vol. 6 (pp. 24–30). Oxford: Elsevier.

Kallis, G., Kerschner, C., & Martinez-Alier, J. (2012). The economics of degrowth. *Ecological Economics* 84: 172–180.

Kallis, G., Schneider, F., & Martinez-Alier, J. (2010). Growth, recession or degrowth for sustainability and equity? *Journal of Cleaner Production* 18(6): 511–606.

Kubiszewski, I., Costanza, R., Franco, C., Lawn, P., Talberth, J., Jackson, T., & Aylmer, C. (2013). Beyond GDP: Measuring and achieving global genuine progress. *Ecological Economics* 93: 57–68.

Latouche, S. (1992). *L'occidentalizzazione del mondo*, Turin: Bollati Boringhieri.

Latouche, S. (1993). *Il pianeta dei naufraghi. Saggio sul doposviluppo*. Turin: Bollati Boringhieri.

Latouche, S. (1995). *I profeti sconfessati. Lo sviluppo e la deculturazione*, Molfetta: La Meridiana.

Latouche, S. (1996). *The westernization of the world*. Cambridge, UK: Polity

Latouche, S. (1997). *L'altra Africa. Tra dono e mercato*, Turin: Bollati Boringhieri.

Latouche, S. (2001). *L'invenzione dell'economia*, Bologna: Arianna Editrice.

Latouche, S. (2007). *La scommessa della decrescita*, Milan: Feltrinelli.

Latouche, S. (2008). *Breve trattato sulla decrescita serena*. Turin: Bollati Boringhieri.

Latouche, S. (2009). *Mondializzazione e decrescita. L'alternativa africana*. Bari: Dedalo.

Latouche, S. (2011). *Vers une société d'abondance frugale: Contresens et controverses de la décroissance*. Paris: Fayard/Mille et une.

Latouche, S. (2011). *Come si esce dalla società dei consumi*. Turin: Bollati Boringhieri.

Latouche, S. (2012). *Per un'abbondanza frugale*. Turin: Bollati Boringhieri

Latouche, S. (2014). Decolonization of imaginary. In G. D'Alisa et al. (Eds.), *Degrowth: A vocabulary for a new era* (pp. 117–120). New York: Routledge.

Latouche, S. (2016). *La decrescita prima della decrescita. Precursori e compagni di strada*. Turin: Bollati Boringhieri.

Latouche, S. (2019). *La décroissance*. Paris: Que sais-je?/Humensis.

Latouche, S., & Romano, O. (2010). Le défi de la décroissance. *Les cahiers européens de l'imaginaire* 2: 62–71.

Lauriola, V. (2013). Indigenous lands, commons, juridical pluralism and sustainability in Brazil: Lessons from the indigenous lands of Raposa Serra do Sol. *Journal of Latin America Geography*. 12(1): 157–185.

Leonardi, E. (2017). *Lavoro, natura e valore. André Gorz tra marxismo e decrescita*. Orthotes: Nocera Inferiore.

McClelland, D. C. (1961). *The achieving society*. New York: The Free Press.

Maffesoli, M. (1998). *Le temps des tribus*. Paris: Table Ronde.

Maffesoli, M. (2004). *Le rythme de la vie*. Paris: Table Ronde.

Maffesoli, M. (2007). *Le réenchantement du monde*. Paris: Table Ronde.

Magatti, M. (2009). *Libertà immaginaria: Le illusioni del capitalismo tecno-nichilista*. Milan: Feltrinelli.

Magatti, M. (2012). *La grande contrazione*. Milan: Feltrinelli.

Magnaghi A. (2010). Crisi ecologica globale e progetto locale. In O. Marzocca (Ed.), *Governare l'ambiente?* (pp. 47–67). Milan: Mimesis.

Mannheim, K. (1991). *Ideology and utopia: An introduction to the sociology of knowledge*. London: Routledge.

Marshall, T. H. (1992). *Citizenship and social class*. London: Pluto.

Martinez-Alier, J. (2002). *The environmentalism of the poor*. Cheltenham, UK: Edward Elgar.

Martinez-Alier, J., Healy, H., Temper, L., Walter, M., Rodriguez-Labajos, B., Gerber, J.-F., & Conde, M. (2011). Between science and activism: Learning and teaching ecological economics with environmental justice organizations. *Local Environment* 16(1): 17–36.

Martinez-Alier, J., Kallis, J., Veuthey, S., Walter, M., & Temper, L. (2010). Social metabolism, ecological distribution conflicts, and valuation languages. *Ecological Economics* 70(2): 153–158.

Marx, K. (1909). *Capital: A critique of political economy*. Chicago: Kerr & Co.

Marx, K. (1964). *Early writings*. New York: McGraw-Hill.

Marx, K. (1973). *Grundrisse: Foundation of the critique of political economy*. New York: Vintage.

Marx, K. (1990). *Capital* (vol. 1). London: Penguin.

Marx, K., & Engels, F. (1963). *German ideology*. New York: International Publishers.

Marx, K., & Engels, F. (1998). *The Communist manifesto*. New York: Monthly Review Press.

Matthey, A. (2010). Less is more: The influence of aspirations and priming on well-being. *Journal of Cleaner Production* 18(6): 567–570.

Mauss, M. (1950). *Essai sur le don*. Paris: Presses Universitaires de France.

Merton, R. K. (1963). *Social theory and social structure.* New York: Free Press of Glencoe.

Merton, R. K. (1996). *On social structure and science.* Chicago: University of Chicago Press.

Mill, J. S. (2015). *On liberty, utilitarianism and other essays.* Oxford: Oxford University Press.

Morin, E. (1971). Préface. In D. Riesman (Ed.), *La foule solitaire* (pp. 5–18). Arthaud: Paris.

Münch, R., & N. J. Smelser (Eds.). (1992). *Theory of culture* (pp. 64–87). Berkeley, CA: University of California Press.

Muraca, B. 2013. 'Décroissance. A project for a radical transformation of society.' *Environmental Values* 22: 147–169

Mylondo, B. (Ed.). (2009). *La décroissance économique: Pour la soutenabilité écologique et l'équité sociale.* Bellecombe-en-Bauges: Éditions du Croquant.

Nebbia, G. (2002). *Le merci e i valori. Per una critica ecologica al capitalismo.* Milan: Jaca Book.

Nebbia, G. (2007). Crescita di chi e di che cosa? *Ecologia Politica,* at www.information guerrilla.org/crescita-di-che-cosa-e-di-chi

Nelson, A., & Schneider, F. (Eds.). (2018). *Housing for degrowth: Principles, models, challenges and opportunities.* New York: Routledge.

Nisbet, R. A. (1996). *The sociological tradition.* London: Transaction.

O'Connor, J. (2002). *The fiscal crisis of the state.* New Brunswick, NJ: Transaction.

Odum, H. T., & Odum, E. C. (2001). *A prosperous way down.* Boulder: University Press of Colorado.

Panikkar, R. (1995). *Reinventare la politica.* Città di Castello: L'Altrapagina.

Pareto, V. (2010). *Trattato di sociologia generale.* Florence: Nabu Press.

Parsons, T. (1991). *The social system.* London: Routledge.

Perkins, P. E. (2019). Climate justice, commons, and degrowth. *Ecological Economics* 160: 183–190.

Petrosino, D., & Romano, O. (2017). *Buonanotte Mezzogiorno.* Rome: Carocci.

Piketty, T., & Goldhammer, A. (2014). *Capital in the twenty-first century.* Cambridge, MA: Belknap Press of Harvard University Press.

Polanyi, K. (2001). *The great transformation. The political and economic origins of our time.* Boston, MA: Beacon Press.

Pörksen, U. (1995). *Plastic words: The tyranny of a modular language.* University Park, PA: Pennsylvania University Press.

Rahnema, M. (2004). *Quand la misère chasse la pauvreté.* Arles: Actes Sud.

Rawls, J. (1999). *A theory of justice.* Harvard, MA: Harvard University Press.

Recalcati, M. (2010). *L'uomo senza inconscio.* Milan: Raffaello Cortina.

Rella, F. (2003). Lo sguardo ulteriore della bellezza. In G. Bataille, *La parte maledetta* (pp. 11–30). Turin: Bollati Boringhieri.

Research & Degrowth. (2010) Degrowth Declaration of the Paris 2008 conference. *Journal of Cleaner Production* 18(6): 523–524.

Riesman, D. (1950). *The lonely crowd.* New Haven, CT: Yale University Press.

Rodotà, S. (2012). *Il diritto di avere diritti.* Rome: Laterza.

Rodríguez-Labajos, B., Yánez, I., Bond, P., Greyl, L., Munguti, S., Uyi Ojo, G., & Overbeek, W. (2019). Not so natural an alliance? Degrowth and environmental justice movements in the global South. *Ecological Economics* 157: 175–184.

Romano, O. (1993). Le illimitate accessibilità del codice tecnologico. *Democrazia e Diritto* 1: 73–88.

Romano, O. (2004). Il postmoderno transadriatico: Per una sociologia immaginaria della periferia appuro-albanese. In F. Botta & I. Garzia (Eds.), *Europa adriatica* (pp. 134–155). Rome: Laterza.

Romano, O. (2008). *La comunione reversiva*. Rome: Carocci.

Romano, O. (2009). Les enjeux anthropologiques de la décroissance. In B. Mylondo (Ed.), *La décroissance économique: Pour la soutenabilité écologique et l'équité sociale* (pp. 169–180). Bellecombe-en-Bauges: Éditions du Croquant.

Romano, O. (2012). How to rebuild democracy, re-thinking degrowth. *Futures* 44(6): 582–589.

Romano, O. (2014). *The sociology of knowledge in a time of crisis: Challenging the phantom of liberty*. New York: Routledge.

Romano, O. (2016). La precarizzazione mobilitante. *Democrazia e Diritto* 1: 65–84.

Rosa, H., & Henning, C. (2017). *The good life beyond growth: New perspectives*. New York: Routledge.

Saed. (2012). Introduction to the degrowth symposium. *Capitalism Nature Socialism* 23(1): 26–29.

Sahlins, M. (1974). *Stone age economics*. London: Tavistock.

Samerski, S. (2018). Tools for degrowth? Ivan Illich's critique of technology revisited, *Journal of Cleaner Production* 197(2): 1637–1646.

Scheler, M. (1960). *Die Wissensformen und die Gesellschaft*. Bern: Francke Verlag.

Schneider, F. (2008). Macroscopic rebound effects as argument for economic degrowth. In *Proceedings of the First International Conference on Economic De-Growth for Ecological Sustainability and Social Equity* (pp. 29–36), Paris.

Schneider, F., Kallis, G., & Martinez-Alier, J. (2010). Crisis or opportunity? Economic degrowth for social equity and ecological sustainability. *Journal of Cleaner Production* 18(6): 511–518.

Schröder, P., Bengtsson, M., Cohen, M., Dewick, P., Hoffstetter. J., & Sarkis. J. (2019). Degrowth within – Aligning circular economy and strong sustainability narratives. *Resources, Conservation and Recycling* 146: 190–191.

Sekulova, F., Kallis, G., Rodríguez-Labajos, B., Schneider, F. (2013). Degrowth: From theory to practice. *Journal of Cleaner Production* 28: 1–6.

Sennett, R. (2006). *The culture of the new capitalism*. New Haven, CT: Yale University Press.

Singh, N. M. (2019). Environmental justice, degrowth and post-capitalist futures. *Ecological Economics* 163: 138–142.

Sorman, A. H., & Giampietro, M. (2013). The energetic metabolism of societies and the degrowth paradigm: Analyzing biophysical constraints and realities. *Journal of Cleaner Production* 38: 80–93.

Sorokin, P. (1985). *Social and cultural dynamics: A study of change in major systems of art, truth, ethics, law, and social relationships*. New Brunswick, NJ: Transaction.

Stoekl, A. (2007). *Bataille's peak: Energy, religion, and postsustainability*. Minnesota: University of Minnesota Press.

Strunz, S., & Bartkowski, B. (2018). Degrowth, the project of modernity, and liberal democracy. *Journal of Cleaner Production* 196: 1158–1168.

Tainter, J. A. (2003). *The collapse of complex societies*. Cambridge, UK: Cambridge University Press.

Tönnies, F. (1963). *Community and society*. New York: Harper & Row.

Vandeventer, J. S., Cattaneo, C., & Zografos, C. (2019). A degrowth transition: Pathways for the degrowth niche to replace the capitalist-growth regime. *Ecological Economics* 156: 272–286.

Veca, S. (1990). *Cittadinanza*, Milan: Feltrinelli.

Victor, P. A. (2012). Growth, degrowth and climate change: A scenario analysis. *Ecological Economics* 84: 206–212.

Von Hayek, F. A. (2006). *Constitution of liberty*. London: Routledge.

Weber, M. (1927). *General economic history*. F. H. Knight (Trans.). New York: Greenberg.

Weber, M. (1947). *The theory of economic and social organization*. New York: Free Press.

Weber, M. (1968). *Economy and society: An outline of interpretative sociology*. New York: Bedminster Press.

Weber, M. (1992). *The Protestant ethic and the spirit of capitalism*. London: Routledge.

Weiss, M., & Cattaneo, C. (2017). Degrowth – Taking stock and reviewing an emerging academic paradigm. *Ecological Economics* 137: 220–230.

Whitehead, M. (2013). Degrowth or regrowth? *Environmental Values* 22: 141–145.

Wilkinson, R., & Pickett, K. (2009). *The spirit level: Why greater equality makes societies*. New York: Bloomsbury.

Wolfe, A. (2001). *Moral freedom: The search of virtue in a world of choice*. New York: Norton.

Xue J. (2014). Is eco-village/urban village the future of a degrowth society? An urban planner's perspective. *Ecological Economics* 105: 130–138.

Zimmermann, D. H., & Pollner, M. (1970). The everyday life as a phenomenon. In *People and information* (pp. 80–103). New York: Pergamon.

Žižek, S. (2001). *On belief*. London: Routledge.

Žižek, S. (2008). *The plague of fantasies*. London: Verso.

Žižek, S. (2009). *First as tragedy, then as farce*. London: Verso.

Index

Printed in the United States
By Baker & Taylor Publisher Services

Printed in the United States
by Baker & Taylor Publisher Services